Saddle to Sailboat

God Bless You

Author: Don Stoderl

1

Editor: Penny Schriver

I want to thank my family and friends in Wyoming and Florida for encouraging me to write about the lady I love.

This is a fictional story based on a real life.

Some names and places are changed.

Chapter "1"

Hey Cowgirl! You want to buy a boat? Are you crazy I shouted! What would I do with a boat on my Wyoming Ranch? Now if you have a horse or a cow for sale we can talk business. He said no, all I have for sale are boats thirty feet long up to one hundred feet long. The day we arrived in Florida until the day we left, all my husband could talk about were boats and the bigger the better. I think he loved boats and the ocean more than he liked food. Maybe that is why he only weighed one hundred and forty five pounds.

That is how my trip to Miami Florida started. My feet were killing me from all the walking in boots that are made for the saddle. My new city guy husband insisted that I see Florida. Now I saw it and I'm ready to go back to Wyoming, God's country. I don't know why anybody would want to live in a state full of mosquitoes, no-see-ums, and alligators. But, my new husband Don, the city guy, said "No, you haven't seen anything yet." The first thing I did was buy a pair of walking shoes. Then we were off to Vicaya Museum and gardens. It was one of the most intricately designed mansions, from the rooms to the gardens that I ever saw.

Next we went to Fairchild Tropical Botanic Garden. It has every kind of plant including palms, flowering trees and vines. It also has varies kinds of Butterflies. Some sat on my arms as we walked and looked at the beautiful flowers.

Then we were off to the Coral Castle. It is truly a remarkable creation. It was made by one man. It is still a mystery how he accomplished it because some pieces weigh over one thousand pounds.

Next was the Miami Zoo. I think they have every kind of animal and bird that ever lived. I enjoyed the monkeys. Some were so cute and some of the birds danced for us.

Parrot Jungle was the best. It's now called Jungle Island. They have over one thousand parrots, some Pink Flamingoes, Cockatoos and many other beautiful birds.

Now it's time to go to Orlando and visit Disney world. Everybody knows about Disney World so what can I say. We spent two days there and had the time of our life with rides and shows.

Sea world was absolutely amazing. There were great shows especially the Sea Lions and the

Dolphins.

From Orlando we went to Melbourne. We walked the beach several times and I picked up a bag of shells that I might or might not ever use.

On Sunday we went to a Baptist church, the church where Don was a member when he lived here. I loved that Church because the Preacher preached in a manner that I could comprehend and the singing was good old songs that everybody knew.

We went fishing on a large boat with four other people and I caught a nice big fish about two feet long. Don informed me that it was a grouper. We cleaned it and cut it up. Cooked some, ate it in our Airstream Trailer and froze the remainder to eat later. That was the best fish I have ever eaten, maybe because it was fresh right out of the ocean.

We also went to the square dance club that Don belonged to before I met him. That almost turned into a disastrous event when he introduced me as his wife to his old square dance partner. Giving me the eagle eye, she said, "I was planning to marry him and now you have taken him away from me." We danced there again the next week and I gave her a beautiful flower that I had crocheted. A few weeks later she gave me a plant that is called a friendship plant. After that we became good friends. She was a lovely lady, but I'm glad she didn't get my man.

We were busy every day going and doing things. We went to about a hundred other places that winter just sightseeing and having fun.

When the winter was over I looked back at everything we did and everything I saw, and I must admit that Florida is not too bad. I'm sure we will be back. I met a lot of nice people and made some very good friends in church, square dancing and in the campground where we stayed. Some wanted us to stop at their homes up north on our way back to Wyoming, and in turn I invited them to my ranch.

I miss good old Wyoming, my ranch, horses, cattle, the animal smells, the peace and tranquility of the country, and my western cowboy and cowgirl friends. I know, too, that it's time to put the cows in the summer pasture. I left my two sons in charge of the ranches and they know what to do but I am looking forward to being back there to oversee and supervise what is being done. I am still a rancher in my heart and all this fun, excitement and a new husband can't take that away from me. It's in my blood. I can't wait to put on my boots, get in my saddle, and on my horse again.

Chapter "2"

I was married to my first husband for forty two years. We were ranchers, cowboy and cowgirl. After he passed away I met this city guy very briefly at an Airstream Travel Trailer Rally in Idaho. A month later we met again by accident at another Airstream Rally in my home town of Douglas, Wyoming. I didn't think we had anything in common, and he was thinking the same thing. I invited him to my small ranch near town. I have a dog at my ranch that doesn't like anybody but family. I thought if my dog liked him he was okay. He came to the ranch and my dog loved him. He stayed in his Airstream for two days and then left for Washington, DC. He had some kind of business in Washington, DC to attend to plus his two Sons and a Daughter lived there.

We dated the old fashioned way. The second night at the ranch I took him to the Senior Center in town to a dance. He told me he didn't like to ballroom dance, but he consented to go. When we arrived they had just started dancing, and all the old widow ladies wanted to dance with him. Being the kind hearted gentleman he is, he danced with all of them, and at the end or the last dance he finally asked me to dance. For a while I thought I had lost him to one of those nice old ladies. I believe that when they went to bed that night they felt ten years younger and had only half of their aches and pains. Had he not danced with them they would have just sat there against the wall in those hard chairs, with empty minds and listened to the music.

He told me that two days at the ranch and with my family was not enough and wished that time permitted him to stay longer.

After he left, my friend Minnie and I flew to Alaska to help my daughter Inez and her family move back to Wyoming from Anchorage. Her husband worked on the north slope of Alaska drilling oil wells. He worked for two weeks then was home for a week. Inez wasn't happy there and wanted to move back to Wyoming. When her husband got a week off, he could just as easily fly to Wyoming instead of Anchorage. On the way to Alaska I told Minnie all I knew about Don. She was as excited for me as I was.

From Washington, DC Don went to the Florida Keys. We wrote letters to each other. In the winter I went to Arizona and lived in my Park Model

Trailer. He came to Arizona and lived in his Airstream at the same park. The more we saw of each other the more we were convinced that we were compatible and could get along with each other the rest of our lives. He told me that he was praying and asking God for a wife for some time and after meeting me twice by accident he was certain God was answering his prayer. Eight months after we met we were married.

He loved to square dance. He not only enjoyed it but was a very good high level dancer. I took lessons and found that I liked it also and I was having as much fun as he was. The first year of our marriage we traveled all over the United States sightseeing, square dancing in all the clubs we could find and getting to know each other better. We danced with local clubs, we danced on or inside of the Hoover Dam, and we danced in a Lake near the shore some place in Arizona, where the water was about ten inches deep, on a large Party Boat, and barefoot in the sand at the lake shore. I discovered the square dancers like to have fun, sometimes I think they are a little crazy. We had loads of fun and met a lot of very nice square dancers who wanted us to stay and dance with them the next time they met. Sometimes it was hard to leave such nice people, but we wanted to move on and spend some time alone. Plus we wanted to see and do more.

When it started to get cool in the northern states Don suggested we spend the winter in Florida. That is the time and place where a boat salesman wanted to sell me a boat.

We spent the following summer at my ranch in Wyoming. Don enjoyed it because it was so different from the life he had previously. He worked as an undercover agent for CIA for seven years, and then worked in the White House for President Kennedy and later for President Johnson. After that he worked at the National Institutions of Health doing Medical Research. He had been in all fifty states and many countries around the world.

I showed him the town where I was born. Dad always teased me saying I was born on the wrong side of the tracks. I told him no, I was born between the tracks. There is a track for trains going east and a track for trains going west. The space between the tracks was about five hundred feet. In the middle was a building called Section House. That is where the track workers slept and ate their meals when they worked in the area. There was no hospital in town at that time, but there was a mid-wife, so they built a maternity room in the far end of the section house. That is where I was born, between the tracks.

Chapter "3"

I asked Don what he would like to see at the ranch. He said he would enjoy whatever I wanted to show him. He also became more acquainted with my four children.

I decided to take him to some of the school houses I attended. Then I asked him if he would like to ride a horse or should we drive the truck. He consented to riding a horse because it sounded very exciting and fun. I added that, it would also be faster and we would see more. My son rounded up two horses and saddled them. We got on the horses and Don's eyes really lit up. He was going to ride a horse for the first time in his life. We started in a trot, and I noticed he was bouncing like a rubber ball. We stopped and he asked me why my horse was moving so smoothly and his was so rough. And why were his ears going back and forth or flicking. I taught him how to ride so he wouldn't bounce and informed him the horse knew it has a stranger on his back. That is why he was moving his ears or flicking them as he had questions. We began our ride and once again he was bouncing. He remarked that the horse just didn't like him. He recalled that when he was young, he worked on a farm and the boss told him, that when a horse has his ears back, it's like a woman who doesn't talk. You know that trouble isn't far ahead. He thought his horse was looking for a nice pile of manure to buck him off and into. Then he asked me, have you ever been bucked off? I told him, "Yes" I was bucked off when my Mother was five months pregnant with me plus many times since and I have bones that weren't set right to prove it. He decided that we should walk the horses back to the barn and take the truck. We took the truck and I showed him some of the school houses I attended, and told him the trouble I went through to go to school.

I started school when I was five years old. Every morning in the winter after a big early breakfast I would stumble through the snow and ride my one eyed horse "Poddy" two and a half miles to a log school house. After school it was another two and a half miles to get home. When it was warm it was better, but it was still very early in the day especially for a five year old girl. During the long winter months it was so early that it was still dark. I had to go through two fence gates to get to school. My Dad made four ladders, one on each side for both fences so I could get on and off my horse. My horse, Poddy, would stop at the first ladder so I could get off. When I had the gate open she would walk through and stop by the next ladder and wait for me to close the gate, and get back on her. It was repeated for the next fence gate. She had a baby that had to stay at the ranch. As I was riding to school she kept looking back to see if she could see her baby, so going to school was slow but going home was much faster because she wanted to be with her baby. She knew her baby was hungry and she needed to feed her.

For some unknown reason the same log school house I previously attended had been moved five miles from my home. Lumber and brick were too expensive and scarce so they just moved the whole schoolhouse rather than build a new one. Mother and Dad felt that I was too young to ride a horse that far to school. That year I stayed with a family friend that lived about half a mile from the school so I could walk to school. The next two and a half years I lived at home again and rode my horse five miles each way to the log school house. By this time I was older and taller so I didn't need the ladders Dad made. It was still hard for me because there were more fence gates to go though. Most of my trip every day was across country. Some fence gates were on our ranch road and some in our pasture because I would cut across. We had auto gates that vehicles drove across but animals will not cross over them. In the summer the road might have mud and in the winter it might have snow and ice.

One winter morning in 1935 it was very cold. I got on my good old one eyed faithful horse and went to school as usual. On the way to school the weather turned into a blizzard. When I arrived at school my fingers, feet and face were frozen. The teacher was not there and only a few of the nine students had arrived. There was no fire in the potbellied stove that sat in the middle of the room. We all went to the teacher's house which was three quarters of a mile away. She thawed me out with snow and sent all of us students back to our homes. My horse was as cold as I was and wanted to get home and in the barn. We went home as fast as she could run in the snow. When I got home I was so cold I couldn't get off my horse. Mother and Dad came out of the house and lifted me off. When my mother saw my condition she said she was not going to put me on a horse again to go to school. I could just stay home and be a live dummy instead of an educated dead girl.

The only option to continue my education was to live with my Dad's sister in another town. I lived there until I finished fifth grade. While living with her I deliver the Denver Post newspaper and the Avon products she sold. I didn't enjoy living there, but I did get an education and also learned to tap dance. My biggest problem was that I was a country girl and was not accepted by the other students. They were city kids and thought themselves too good for me.

For sixth and seventh grade I rode my horse two and a half miles to a bus stop. Before I left home I would always let my horse drink all the water he wanted because to and from school was before sun up to after sun down. When I got to the bus stop I would tether my horse on a long staked rope so he could graze on grass while I was in school. There was a big cottonwood tree there so he could stand in the shade after he had enough to eat. Then I rode the bus for fifteen miles to a country school. The school had one teacher and eight students.

For my eighth grade Mother and I lived in town. Mother got a job as a housekeeper and baby sitter and I went to school and tried to be a town girl instead of a rancher tomboy/cowgirl. We went to the ranch as often as we could. I always looked forward to that so I could be with my Dad, my horse, her colt, my cat and my dog. As soon as I got home allW my animal friends and I started running, jumping, and playing. I was an only child so all my friends and playmates on the ranch were animals. Every year my horse had a colt for me to play with and spoil. In the summer when there was no school, there were times when Mother and Dad would go to town to shop and I would stay home. That is when I would bring my colt into the house for a little sugar and show him where I slept. After that he always wanted to come in our house. I think Mother and Dad knew why.

I remember when I was about five years old I was under my horse, Poddy, playing with my dog Fuzz. My horse lifted her leg to chase away some flies. Then she was afraid to put her foot down because she knew I was under her. Later my mother saw it and told me to get away from the horse so she could put her foot down. I don't know how long my horse stood there on three legs before my mother saw it.

For my freshman year I stayed in a private home with a girl named Minnie who was also a freshman. She and I became lifelong friends and to this day we talk on the phone and write to one another. In my last year of high school we leased the ranch to a nice couple that did a good job managing it. Mother and Dad bought a motel in town and we all moved to town and to become a family again. Before I went to school I had to wash the guest's bed sheets and pillow cases and hang them on a line to dry. When I came home after school I would take them off the line and Mother would iron them using a mangle. I only had twelve blocks to walk to school there. That was so nice and easy. I also started to wear fashionable town clothes. For a while I enjoyed my town life but it didn't take long and I began to miss all my animal friends from the ranch. All I had with me in town was my faithful dog "Fuzz." In the daytime I went to school and after school I worked a part time job as a telephone operator on the town switchboard, working from four to midnight. When work got slow around ten I could study and do my homework. Working on the switchboard was very educational for me because I learned so much about that kind of work and people. After I finished school the government built a prisoner of war camp in our area and I worked in a civil service position as a telephone switchboard operator. Mother and Dad also were hired at the camp. Mother was a cook and Dad was a repair and maintenance worker. Mother was always a good cook, and Dad, being a rancher fifty miles out of town learned to fix and repair anything that needed repairing.

Chapter "4"

Living in town eventually spoiled me. We lived in a very nice house with designer furniture, good water pressure, electricity and an indoor bathroom with a bath tub. Compared to ranch living this was like heaven to us.

On the ranch we lived in a log house, our homestead house. The floor was made with pine boards. The ceiling was tar paper and layered on top of that was corrugated sheets of metal topped with sod. We had a kitchen, a combined living and dining room and one bedroom. Mother and Dad slept in the bedroom and I slept in the opposite end of our house. I had a curtain that I pulled across the room to separate me from the rest of the house. We had a wood and coal burning stove in the kitchen and a big potbellied stove in the center of the house which kept us warm in the winter. Our kitchen stove had a reservoir on the end. The fire in the stove heated the water so we had hot water all the time. One of my chores was to keep water in the reservoir.

On the stove was a large coffee pot with grounds in it that were probably as old as I was.

Dad never changed the grounds; he just added more coffee grounds to the grounds already in the pot. When I was about ten years old I planned to surprise Dad and clean his coffee pot. When I was finished it was shiny, and looked like new. I was so proud of myself but when Dad came home and saw what I had done, his face turned bright red and puffy. I knew then I should not have touched his coffee pot. I ruined both his coffee and the pot. I didn't know it at the time but washing and cleaning his coffee pot was a hanging offense. If he would have had a rope handy he would have thrown it over a rafter and I would have been a dead duck. That day I learned a very important lesson; don't ever mess with a cowboy's coffee or his coffee pot.

In the dining room we had a large handmade table with a chair at each end and a bench on each side.

We had some coal on our ranch so before winter blasted in, Dad would hook a team of horses to the wagon and haul in a few loads for the kitchen and living room stoves. Every winter Dad had to chink the cracks between the logs in our house with straw mixed with clay mud and cow manure to keep the wind and snow out. We had no electricity or telephone service. For light we had three kerosene/oil lamps. Years later Dad made a six volt wind charger. Then we had one bare electric blub hanging in the kitchen, one in the living-dining room and one in their bedroom. The wires ran from the wind charger through the wall of our log home and then ran along the ceiling to the bare bulbs that dangled from the ceiling of each room. On the walls we had wooden pegs where we hung our coats, hats and other items. Hanging on the walls were several deer heads with big antlers to hold rifles and a shot gun. Mother and I could shoot as well as Dad. We had to be good shots because ammunition was expensive and we depended on wild animals for our meat. We had beef and mutton but it was to sell not to eat.

Our privy was a little house out back and away from our log house. It was always equipped with a Sears and Roebuck catalog. You never stayed in it longer than necessary. In the winter it was freezing and in the summer it was hot as an oven.

For some years we carried water from a well which was on a hill about a thousand feet from our house. We had a twenty gallon barrel in the kitchen, and it was my job to keep that barrel full of water. It was a big job until Dad put a tank and a windmill at the well. Then later he put in a pipe to run water from the tank to the house. After that we always had gravity fed running water in our house.

Every summer we had a huge garden. We ate fresh vegetables all summer and had enough to can that would last all winter. We also canned chicken, pork and deer meat.

In the fall of the year Dad would buy a big fat pig. We butchered it and cut it up on the ranch as we did with all the animals we ate. Some of the meat we salted and some we canned. The fat or lard was melted down and boiled. Then we added lye (an alkaline solution) to make soap. Sometimes that soap was used on the hands but most of it was used as laundry soap. We used every part of the pig for something except the squeal.

We kept one milking cow near our house. Her name was Goldie. Every morning and every evening Mother or I would milk Goldie. We had a separator machine that separated the cream from the milk. When we needed butter we would let the cream get a little sour, and then put it in a covered wooden pail with a hole on top. There was a paddle with a long handle that went through the cover hole.

Then we would pull the handle up and down until we had butter. It took about thirty minutes. We also made cottage cheese. We put skim milk in a crock container and let it clabber.(sour milk that has thickened or curdled) Then it was put on the back part of the stove where it was always warm until the cottage cheese was the right consistency.

To keep the milk, cream and butter cold we put it in a container with a tight cover and lowered it down the well and into the cold water. The water was so cold that getting a swallow of it in the summer heat was very refreshing.

We washed our clothes in a washing machine that had a handle on the side. As we pulled the handle back and forth the agitator would go back and forth to wash the clothes. For soap we grated a third of a bar of the lye soap we made from our pig fat. The machine had rollers on top with a crank you turned to squeeze the water out of the wet clothes. Later Dad bought a small gasoline engine that he mounted under the machine so we didn't have to pull the handle back and forth or turn the crank. It was a bizarre contraption but it worked saving us time and muscle power. We hung the clothes on a line outside to dry by the sun and a little wind. When we put them on they smelled so good and clean from being dried by fresh air. In the winter they froze on the line but they got dry. The wind would keep them soft so you could fold them.

Chapter "5"

Because we lived fifty miles from town we only went to town about once a month if the road was not all mud or there was too much snow. Before we bought our pickup truck we went in a wagon pulled with a team of horses. We would leave home at sun up with milk, cream, butter and eggs to sell and trade. In the summer it was all packed with ice that Dad cut from our dike last winter. Some we sold to families' that had a standing order. The remainder we traded at the grocery store for coffee, sugar, flour and other items we didn't raise or grow on our ranch. It would take all day to get to town and sell and trade our product. While Mother and I were selling and trading, Dad would go into the general merchandise store to meet his friends. They would sit and talk, tell stories and I'm sure they stretched the truth a little to keep their stories interesting. They would roll a handmade cigarette from a sack of Bull Durham or a can of Velvet tobacco into cigarette papers or smoke their pipes. If they had a pipe they would relight it every five or ten minutes. Every man carried a little box of stick matches in his pocket. They would light the match by striking it on anything nearby or on their pants leg to light their pipe or cigarette. Some would eat a five cent dill pickle from the pickle barrel along with a free cracker. They all carried a jack knife in their pocket and some would start to whittle on a piece of wood. After some time they would gravitate to the bar, saloon or beer joint. Whatever you want to call it, the end results were always the same. Too much liquor and then a fist fight. I don't know if it was what cowboys did in those days or if it was the liquor, but if Dad didn't get into a fight he felt the trip to town was wasted. We stayed overnight in town, shopped the next day and went home. In the winter we went to town only a few times because it was too cold. When we would go, we wrapped blankets around us, but we still got cold.

After we purchased our pickup truck, we would do it all in one day but arrived home well after dark. It was always too dark to find our milk cow and so she didn't get milked until the next morning. Once a year she had a baby that we kept in the barn. When we were home the calf would get half of the milk and we would get the other half. When we planned to go to town we would keep some milk aside to feed her calf when we got home.

Going to town and shopping was always a special treat for me. The one place I remember very well was a store with a big barrel full of dill pickles. On the side was a large long fork. If you wanted a pickle, you just stuck the fork into one, pulled it out and ate it right there. I think it cost five cents. The one big thing I really enjoyed was eating in a restaurant. There were so many different items of food to choose from. Mother was a very good cook but restaurant food was uncommonly different and good plus I didn't have to help prepare it or wash dishes.

Chapter "6"

Don remarked, you have had a hard life so far and you were still very young. Why did you live out here and how did your Dad get this place? First, I love it out here and second, in 1916 Dad and his brothers each homesteaded a ranch out here. The government gave each of them three hundred and twenty acres. If they improved the acreage, built a home and started to raise cattle or crops, then the government would give them three hundred and twenty acres more. Some built their homes with logs and others dug into the side of a hill for part of their home and the remainder was built with logs or stone and mud. They also had to dig wells, not only for their own use but for the cattle too. They all tried to build their homes and improve the land but times were hard. The ground was hard and dry. His brothers and some neighbors couldn't find work and were going hungry. They just could not get started building a ranch. Before they starved they started selling their land. Six hundred and forty acres were not enough land in that part of the country to make a living even in good times. Some of the land was selling from fifty cents to two dollars an acre. My Mother and Dad started to buy some of the homesteads that were really cheap. They used the money they had saved from working at other ranches miles away where the grass grew plus money they earned selling their chickens, turkeys, eggs, milk, cream and butter. Because Mother and Dad were very frugal with their money and with Dad's good reputation, he was able to borrow some money from the bank.

In the 1930's and early 1940' times were very hard again. We had a drought plus the depression days hit us hard. In the late 1930's the cattle and sheep had nothing to eat and were starving. The government passed a bill that gave the ranchers five to seven dollars for each cow and two dollars for each sheep. When the rancher was paid the government men came out and shot all the cows and sheep. Even our milk cow "Goldie" had to be shot. She not only produced our milk, cream and butter, but she was my pet, and they shot her anyway. I cried for a week but it did no good. She was gone.

Mother and Dad worked for other ranchers and anyplace they could find work and for any amount of money. Most of the time it was only a dollar a day and food and the food was mostly beans, antelope or horse meat. Mother and Dad always worked somewhere and saved every cent they earned. They worked on large established ranches and most of the time they were miles away where the grass was still green and growing. Wherever they worked, they always took me with them. Dad was very good at shearing sheep and breaking horses, so he always had a Job. Dad also rode bucking bronc horses in rodeos and state fairs for pay, and Mother would race her horse against other horses. When Dad was to sore from riding bucking horses he would work as a clown. He rode my little Shetland pony, Jerry, with my dog, Fuzz, behind him. His act was always a hit, a real crowd pleaser.

As time went on he bought seven and a half homesteads. Later when the grass started to grow again he bought some cows and a bull. As they multiplied we bought some sheep. Some say that cattle and sheep cannot live together. They are wrong. Sheep will eat the weeds and grass that cattle will not touch. Sheep pay off twice a year. First they have their lambs and second, after they are sheared for their wool.

We had some water wells but had to dig more and put windmills on them. If cows and sheep have to walk more than three miles for water they use up the fat they gained. Mother, Dad and I had a lot of work to do then but we got another start in ranching.

I spent a lot of time herding the cattle and sheep because we didn't have fences yet. Coyotes were plentiful and bad for the sheep. Once when I was herding the sheep a coyote sneaked right into the middle of my sheep before I knew it. When I noticed what was going on, I headed the sheep for home with the coyote in the middle. We were all running as fast as we could and the coyote was snapping at their feet trying to bring one down. He was trying so hard to get one that he wasn't watching where we were going. When we got home we stopped and the coyote realized what was happening. He jumped up and headed back where he came from. I chased him on my Shetland pony until he was out of my sight.

Dad started breaking wild horses at home and shearing sheep for other ranchers. Mother and I milked cows, raised orphan lambs, and raised chickens and turkeys. When the chickens and turkeys got big enough we would butcher them and sell them in town to individuals and stores. Every month or so Dad would go away for a while to get wild unbroken horses. Then another kind of work started. He would break them to ride, and I would work and train them to neck rein (guide or steer), to cut cattle (separate) and to rope from the horse. I was bucked off a few times but I always got back on and worked them until they were well trained. That was a lot of work but I enjoyed it. When I finished training them to work cattle Dad would sell them to ranchers. Then he would get more wild horses and the process started all over again.

Chapter "7"

At certain times of the year we had to hire men to help with our ranch work. They were always hard working men, friendly and good to me. One hired man gave me a two and a half dollar gold coin. Another carved an eagle head in a sheep bone and gave it to me.

There were always fences to build or repair and corrals to build or repair and cattle to work. They also helped with round up. Before all the ranches were fenced the cattle would walk, eat and drink water wherever they could find it. At round up time all the ranchers and hired men gathered all of the cattle and trailed them to the rail head. At the rail head they would be separated by brand and each rancher would sell their own cattle. All cattle, horses and sheep had to be branded. That is still the law today. Our hired men had a comfortable room in the barn where they would sleep and Mother would wash their clothes with ours. They ate their meals in our home as part of our family. Mother always told them one rule we had. When you are finished eating you must carry your plate and silverware to the kitchen or leave twenty five cents under the plate. I never found a quarter or a dirty plate. That rule also continued at my ranch for many years later.

Chapter "8"

When I was about ten years old I was in our pasture working the cattle and I noticed my neighbor and friend across the fence about a mile away. I rode my horse along the fence line until I found a gate. I opened the gate, and went through to visit my friend Ruth. Ruth was about seventeen and big for her age. Ranchers and their children always talk about their horses. Ruth was riding on a beautiful little Shetland pony and I was on Poddy's baby, Sparky, a full grown horse at that time. I noticed that Ruth's feet were only a foot or two from the ground. "Do you want to trade horses?" She answered yes. We traded horses but did not change saddles or bridles. Her little Shetland pony was so cute and friendly. His name was Jerry. I really loved him because he was so small and cute. We had a nice visit after which I went back to our ranch and started working again, this time on my new horse. When I got home Dad inquired, where did you get that horse and where is Sparky? I answered, "I traded horses with Ruth." He said, I can't believe my ten year old girl would trade a good horse for that little thing. I told him I did it because Jerry was so cute and friendly. Dad assured me I would never be a horse trader, but he let me keep him. He was my special horse for many years. Ruth and I have been lifelong friends and for years after that we talked about the time we traded horses. Ranch children grew up fast because there was always work for them to do according to their age. Most of the time they did work that was more appropriate for a person a few years older.

Chapter "9"

I always enjoyed exploring the ranch. I started that at about age seven. I would always take along a lunch and a canteen of water. Then I would get on Poddy and in later years Jerry, put Fuzz on behind me and away we would go. We did that about once a month in the summer, just go and ride. Sometimes I would stop at an ant hill and pick up Ant Money. The harvester ants collect seeds from cactus, sagebrush and other plants. They use it for food and also place it on top of their ant hill. It is about one quarter inch in diameter and one thirty second inch thick with a ridge around the top. It is mostly found in the western states and is pink, blue or red.

On one of my rides out on the ranch I found a sandstone formation that looked like a castle. I could walk about six feet into it. Inside there was a stone shelf. Fuzz and I would play in there for a while and then I got back on Poddy and rode some more. I often wished that I had a brother or sister but because I didn't Poddy, Fuzz and my other pets were my only confidants. There were always beautiful, very small flowers in the grass that I thought would look so lovely in my sandstone castle. The next time Fuzz and I rode Poddy out there I took a little jar along. I picked some flowers, put them in the jar and then took them to my little castle where I put them on the shelf. Poddy was eating grass but every few minutes she would look in at us from the front or top of the formation. The top was mostly open. When Fuzz and I were finished playing I took the flowers home and showed them to my mother. She identified each one of them for me. From then on I had a desire to learn the names of plants. When I went out in the pasture with Mother or Dad I would ask them the name of plants.

I always enjoyed walking out in the pasture with Mother for a mile or two and just talk "girl talk" or about what we saw. Mother was very intelligent and knew the names of all the plants, snakes, little animals, tiny creatures or critters and insects on the ranch. She had enough education to teach school but she never did. She taught me things I didn't learn in school. When Jerry or Poddy, Fuzz and I would go out riding I would tell Fuzz the name of things we saw.

Today, years later I still remember the names of most plants, snakes, little animals, little critters and insects we have on the ranch. I also think about the children of today. Do they know what I know and do they have the fun I had with my pets and just riding out in the wide open spaces.

Parents in those days didn't worry about their children when they were out horseback riding for hours and miles away. Children knew how to work the cattle and how to enjoy their free time. Ranch children had their own horses and dogs. They were tough, dependable and responsible children.

Dad wanted a baby boy when I was born. Because I was a girl, he taught me how to be a boy. But Mother was thrilled I was a girl and taught me how to be a lady. I had the best Mother and Dad anyone could have.

Chapter "10"

When it was time to shear the sheep Dad needed four men. He hired two that went from ranch to ranch shearing. The third one he got from town that was semi-retired. He had fourteen year old son who was invited to join the shearers if he wanted a job. Dad was the fourth member of the shearing team. He informed all three that shearing began at sun up and ended at sun down.

The day before shearing, Dad and I got all the sheep in from the pasture and had them ready for shearing. The two regular shearers arrived before sun up. The man from town was an hour late. Was Dad angry! In a gruff voice he told him, "you lost one hour of work." I'm sure the message came through loud and clear because he knew Dad. His fourteen year old son did come with him. Dad told his son and me to keep the chute full so the shearers could just grab one when they finished shearing the one they had. His son's name was Fred. I told him what to do and that it was time to start. For half an hour he just stood around and was in my way. I suggested he get to work or go sit in his truck. I think he did not take kindly to being ordered around by a ten or twelve year old and especially a ten or twelve year old girl! He gave me some piercing, sarcastic and smart back talk. I invited him to go behind the truck and say that, and I started walking. When I got behind the truck I stopped and turned around. A few seconds later he came and I hit him in his smart mouth with my fist. Then I hit him a few more times until he fell down. I jumped on top of him and started hitting him. We rolled and hit each other until the chute was empty of sheep. Dad hollered for us and asked us why the chute was empty? We couldn't answer because we were actually fighting. Dad came looking for us. When he found us, he picked us up by our shirts, held us about six inches off the ground, and asked, what is going on here? I told him everything. He asked Fred, if I told the truth? Fred knew better than to lie to my Dad. He just said "Yes Sir". Dad warned him, to do what Irene told him to do or start walking back to town. I repeated what to do." Get busy or start walking." He worked hard the rest of that day and didn't say a word about his black eye and bloody lip. I was dirty and had scratches from rolling around on the rough ground but no black eye or cut lip. A few years later we went to the same school and he would never look at me. I never told the other students that I beat him up.

Chapter"11"

One time a male calf was born that its mother couldn't feed or take care of because her bag was infected. I took it and fed it milk from a pail and made a pet out of it. I named him Duffy. When it was old enough, Dad made it a steer. He let me keep it for a pet. I broke it for a saddle and rode it all over the ranch. One day when Fuzz and I took Jerry out for a ride Duffy followed us. Every half hour he would come up alongside of Jerry. I knew then he was jealous and wanted me to ride on him. I took the saddle off Jerry, put it on Duffy and rode him until we got home. Fuzz was never on Duffy before and Duffy didn't like it one bit so I put Fuzz back on Jerry and the two of them followed Duffy and me home.

When it was time to trail or walk some steers and old cows to market, I rode my steer while Dad and his cowboys rode their horses. When we got to the rail head (train station) Dad ordered me to get that saddle off the steer and get it on the train. I cried because it was my pet and I lost both the argument and my steer. All I could do was square my shoulders, get on a horse to ride home.

Chapter"12"

Life wasn't all work. About once a month we would have a dance party at someone's ranch. Some came by road on horseback or wagon and others came across ranches and through fence gates on horseback or wagon. There was food, liquor, music and loads of fun. I learned how to tap dance in school so half way through the evening I would tap dance and onlookers would give me money. I was only about ten or eleven years old then.

Dad was a rough, tough cowboy but he could be mischievous. He enjoyed doing something funny or pulling a joke, but one time he went almost too far. Most of the ranchers had a baby they brought along to the party. One time before the party was over Dad switched the clothes two babies wore. When the parents got home they found they had the wrong baby. Both parents were so angry they could have killed my Dad. Both couples were tired, half drunk and the ranches being miles apart. The men thought about keeping the babies overnight and exchange them the next morning when it was light but the mothers would not hear of it. They wanted their babies back. There were no telephones or radios in those days but by coincidence the two couples met about half way between their respective ranches. The switch was made the middle of the night and the mothers were especially happy.

When I was about six months old my mother was riding her horse carrying me in front of her going to a dance at some ranch. It was dark and her horse stepped in a prairie dog hole and fell. Mother fell off and broke her arm. I was not hurt but for several weeks Mother could not pin a diaper on me so a hired man had to do it. Another hired man taught me to walk. You could say that I had three mothers since all three took care of me plus doing the ranch work. The man that changed my diaper lived in the area for as long as I can remember and every time he would see me he would ask "do you need a clean diaper little girl?" I got so angry at him for saying that but I loved him for helping my Mother and for keeping me dry. Dad had been away for some time shearing sheep and breaking horses. The pay he received for that kind of work was twice as much as he was paying the two hired men.

At another party a single rancher got so drunk he passed out and fell on the floor of our log house.

Mother pulled his boots off and left him lying on the hard floor. In the morning he woke up, put his boots on, got on his horse and went home to his log shack without speaking a word.

Some ranchers had their own still and others made their own beer. Wherever you went there was always plenty of liquor to drink. A couple single men had a large still some miles away from our ranch house. They sold their liquor to anybody that wanted it even to people in the surrounding towns. That went on for eight or ten years before they were caught. They also were caught stealing and butchering one of our cows to eat. Knowing my Dad, I would bet he beat them both up really bad before he called the Sheriff. They went to jail for both offences.

Chapter "13"

One time Dad brought home a string of horses. He had a Pinto pony, a Shetland and Arabian cross/mix. The Pinto Pony was a beautiful little pony with a sweet disposition. I fell in love with him right away. We called him Herbie, the name of his former owner. He was so gentle that he became another one of my pets. After we worked and trained him all spring Dad sold him like he did with all the horses after they were trained. He sold Herbie to a young man named Bob, who worked with his Dad lambing and shearing sheep, locally known as a dollar a day cowboy. I was very unhappy that my pet, my sweet horse Herbie was sold to someone who might not love him and take care of him as I did.

Bob's parents, whom I didn't know at the time, ran an ad in the paper offering a room in their home for a student. Many town people and people that lived near town opened their homes to help country kids receive an education. I stayed there for one year of school and was able to see my Herbie only once because Bob had a job some miles away working on a ranch with sheep and cattle. He came home one weekend and we got acquainted but we had very little in common because he was six years older than I. To me, that six year age difference was a life time. He had a full time job and I was still in school. I did keep in touch with him though because he had my Herbie. He once told me that when he worked on the cattle and sheep ranch that he was paid a dollar a day with room and board. That was the standard pay in those days and room could be in a bunk house or in the barn. He was lucky and had a room in the house. After three months he quit his job and with the ninety dollars he was paid he spent eighty of it on a saddle, and with the ten he had left he used to put a down payment on a friendship ring for me. It was a beautiful saddle that we still have, and as it turned out years later, the friendship ring he gave me became my engagement ring.

When the Japanese bombed Pearl Harbor, Bob joined the Army Air Corps and his dad kept Herbie.

My parents were friends with Bob's parents. When they went there to visit one Sunday afternoon I went with them to see my Herbie.

When we arrived I asked Bob's dad if he would mind if I rode Herbie. He said. Sure you can ride him. He should be in the pasture somewhere and he needs to be ridden and run. He and the other horses just lay around getting fat and lazy. I started walking in the pasture and calling for Herbie. About a mile or more into the pasture he heard me and started running toward me. We were really happy to see each other. He nuzzled me all over and I hugged his neck. I jumped on his back and said, "Go to the barn and we'll get a saddle." He started for the barn with me on his bare back and without a bridle. We were "one" again. After I put a saddle and bridle on him we cantered, trotted and galloped for about an hour. Then we came to a working windmill. We stopped and both had a very cold drink of the best water I tasted in a long time. When we were back at home I took off his saddle and bridle and he rolled on both sides. It felt so good to him. Then I found a curry comb and brush and cleaned him until he shone like a new born colt. He and I thoroughly enjoyed ourselves that afternoon.

Chapter "14"

Bob wanted to be a pilot but the military wouldn't let him because he had an eye defect that would not allow him to land a plane. He went to school to learn how to operate and repair radios. He also was trained to be a noise gunner on a B-24. When his training was completed he and the crew of a B-24 were sent to England for additional training and to stand by for the D-day invasion. While training in England, he was hit in the eye with a pellet and was sent to the local military hospital where he had to keep a sand bag on each side of his head. It was very painful and he was hoping that the doctors could save his sight. There must have been a doctor shortage because he was not properly cared for while hospitalized. He was there almost two weeks waiting to get on a Med-Evac plane to the Fort Lewis Military Hospital. The doctors there were excellent and could have saved his sight and eye if he had been transferred there earlier. By this time he had an infection in his bad eye and nearly lost sight in both eyes but thank God they could at least save one eye. Before he was transferred to the states his crew came to visit him after their first mission. They told him that they took a lot of shrapnel in their plane but no one was hurt. They brought some shrapnel to show him and gave him the details about the mission. He found out later that on their second trip they were shot down and there were no survivors. Bob said that he thanked God for the loss of his eye and not of his life. I wrote to him for quite some time and was beginning to know him quite well. He came home on furlough a few times during the healing process. We came to know each other much better in person because he had plenty of time to talk. Each time he came home he was feeling much better but continued to need intensive eye surgery and treatment. One time while home he wanted to ride Herbie. It had been a long time since he had been on a horse but he was still a cowboy. We put the saddle and bridle on Herbie and Bob got on him. Bob wanted Herbie to run. Herbie ran for about five seconds and stopped. Bob kicked him to make him run and again Herbie ran for about five seconds and stopped. Bob then realized that Herbie knew his medical condition and that he should not be riding. Herbie was right because Bob said his eye and head were starting to hurt. We removed the saddle and bridle and Herbie ambled away about ten feet and stopped. As Bob and I started walking, Herbie followed behind us as if he were a medical aid keeping watch over Bob.

Chapter "15"

Although Bob still had a patch over his eye, we were married the third of September 1944. We had a very short honeymoon in Yellowstone National Park. A few days later he had to leave again because he was being transferred to Dibble General Hospital near Menlo Park in California. At that hospital they fitted him for a glass eye. Because we were married I could go with him. We went by Greyhound bus from Douglas Wyoming to Menlo Park. The bus stopped at every city and small town. It took approximately four or five days to get there. I stayed in a private home near the hospital so I could walk to the hospital to visit with him every day. The couple I stayed with was very congenial and very good to me. They offered to take me wherever I needed to go. Military hospitals at that time did not have individual rooms for their patients, just large open bays. Some patients had more serious and painful war injuries than Bob. I talked with and visited with those that were close to his bed. They all had a good positive attitude and outlook on life. They talked about going home to their wives or girlfriends and starting life over again. When Bob received his glass eye he looked like his original self again. He was sent home for two weeks to continue healing and to get accustomed to his new eye.

Because he was still in the Air Force he was sent to Lowry Air Base in Denver Colorado. We found a nice apartment near the base. I had to find a job to help pay the bills for food and rent. The war was still on and work was plentiful. I got a good job at the Denver Chicago Trucking Company as a receptionist. It was a large company but in an area that didn't look safe. I enjoyed my work and was well paid. When it was time to leave work, I would stay inside the building until I saw the city bus come and then I would run out to board the bus. After one week the driver told me to stay in the building until he came to the bus stop. He would stop and wait for me and also survey the area to make certain it was safe. Bob's job at the base was radio repair. He had to work very slowly and had trouble seeing small items with only one eye. Working with only one eye was a new experience for him, an experience that he sorely needed because that was the way his life would be going from then on. He began learning to do things differently than he had before. He was right handed but found that doing some things left handed worked better, such as shooting a rifle and chopping wood for the stove. It was not long until he was doing everything with both his right and left hand. A few months later the war ended and he was honorably discharged.

Chapter "16"

What happened to Herbie while Bob was gone? He stayed on the ranch with Bob's parents. Now I had Herbie and Bob, the two things that I loved and missed while I was away from them. Some friends jokingly said I married Bob to get Herbie back. That is not true. I married Bob because I loved him, but it was through Herbie that I met Bob.

Bob was discharged in the spring and we decided to live with Bob's parents until we found jobs. Within a week we found a job lambing, herding and shearing sheep. We lived in a sheep wagon for two months away from everyone and everything. You could say it was our second honeymoon. The sheep wagon was about seven feet wide and fourteen feet long. We entered in the front by stepping on the tongue. On the right was a wood burning cook stove, eighteen inches wide by eighteen inches deep with an oven under it. Next to the stove was a work counter and under it was storage. In the rear was a bed four feet wide and six and one half feet long. On the left was a cabinet for food storage and a few pots and pans. Clothes were hung or stored wherever there was room. We carried water from the well that had a windmill and washed dishes and bathed outside.

I had an orphan lamb that I bottle fed. He lived with us in that little sheep wagon so I could take care of him. He was my new pet. He slept under our bed at night next to our shoes and clothes. In the daytime he followed me wherever I went. Now I have two pets, Herbie and a lamb. We also had a big mean dog but he stayed with the sheep and kept the coyotes away.

At lambing time Bob would put a tent in the middle of the sheep to sleep in during the time the sheep were having their little ones. Sometimes they needed help having their lambs or the mother sheep would die. There were times, too, when a first time mother would just walk away from her baby after she bore it. When that occurred, an old mother ewe sheep would mother it and stop having her own baby. Most of the time you could not make the young mother accept her baby if she didn't want it. Sheep are very unusual animals. It has been said that they live to die and some do just lie down and die for no reason.

When the work with the sheep ended we moved in with my mother and dad on the ranch. We made a small bedroom in the opposite end of our log house, where I use to sleep. We helped Dad with his cattle and assisted in the building of and repair the corrals and fences.

In the fall of that year Bob started college under the G I bill. He went to the University of Wyoming in Laramie. While there I worked at a Firestone Auto Parts store in Laramie. It was a large building with a partition in the middle and a six foot walk-through. One half of the building was auto parts and the other half was a general store. The general store sold tools, electrical parts horse bits, saddles and every size screw and bolt, but no food or candy. I missed the pickle barrel but its days had passed. I enjoyed working in both stores, no matter where the boss needed me.

We lived on campus in an eight by twenty foot trailer furnished by the government for veterans who were enrolled in the university. He studied vocational agriculture and did very well in all his studies except algebra. He couldn't pass algebra so after two years he quit.

We returned to the ranch and started buying it from Mother and Dad. We enjoyed living in the country with all the peace and solitude. We became ranchers. The ranch was big enough to raise our cattle and Dad's so we worked together. Dad and Bob bought Hereford cattle and I bought Black Angus with the money I had been saving. Mine always wanted to go back home where they originally came from. Every day for a month I had to run them down by horseback and return them to our ranch. In the spring when the cows had their calves, Dad and Bob had trouble with sunburned utters/bags because they were white. The cows would not let their calves nurse because it was painful for them. They had to hobble (tie the back legs) of each cow until the calf had finished eating. There were times during the calving season that it took all day because they had a lot of cows. They put a medical salve on the cow's bags and after a week or so the cow would let her calf nurse. I had no trouble with mine because the bags on my cows were black. The next year Dad and Bob sold their Hereford cows and bought Black Angus cows.

We lived in the log house and worked as a

family with Mother and Dad for two years. It might sound like it was close quarters but there was so much work to do at the ranch that we were together only in the evenings.

Chapter "17"

One day Dad went to the town of Keeline Wyoming and bought a one bedroom house. That was a surprise to us and we wondered how in the world will he get it to the ranch. When I asked him he just said, "You will see in a few days."

In a few days there it was, coming down the ranch road, bumpity bump through potholes and washed out crevices. He had paid someone to load and transport it on a very large trailer all the way to our ranch which was about ninety five miles. Part of the road was hard top but most of it was ranch or country roads. The roads were rough and narrow. In several places they had to remove the fence and gates. It was a house for Bob and me! What a wonderful surprise! Sometime later we added two more bedrooms and a bathroom with a toilet that drained into a septic tank. The six volt wind charger was too small for both homes so we increased it to thirty two volts. Then we had to build a sixty foot high tower near our house so the wind charger would catch more wind. We also installed a large LP gas (liquefied petroleum) tank near the house.

So now we had gas to cook with, a gas stove for heat in the winter, and a gas water heater to heat water. We also had a gas refrigerator but we still had no telephone or one hundred and twenty volt electricity at our ranch yet. We had water in our house from the same well as the log house. Both were supplied by gravity from the tank on the hill.

Mother and Dad lived in the log house and we continued to ranch and eat together as a family. In addition to the cattle, Bob and I started raising turkeys and chickens. That new enterprise was enough to keep us busy. We built a chicken house so the chickens had protection from wild animals at night and a place to lay their eggs. The turkeys roosted on the corral fence, and if it rained or stormed they would go under the shed. We could always tell when a storm was coming because the turkeys would go under the shed. We sold turkeys and chickens for their meat and also sold chicken eggs to people and stores in town.

Before our first child was born I had lots of work to do in preparation. Mother was a big help in telling me what I needed. Frist I bought enough flannel cloth to make twenty diapers. I cut them in squares and hemmed the edges. Then I bought twelve baby bottles, baby clothes and blankets. Our son Louis was born and two years later our daughter Hazel was born. Now I really had my hands full but the diapers, bottles and other items I used for Louis I could use for Hazel.

Bob and Dad stayed busy with the cattle and repairing or building corrals and fences. The corrals and fences always needed repair. It was a never ending job. We also had to have more wells dug or repaired and windmills installed or repaired. When the work was finally completed, Dad and Mother decided to buy a house in town. We helped them move but it also made more work for Bob and me on the ranch because Dad was always a big help when he was with us.

Chapter "18"

Mother and Dad enjoyed life in town but it didn't take long for Dad to become bored. He bought a truck to haul cattle and sheep to the market for ranchers in the area. Some trips were for shipping cattle and sheep to slaughter houses miles away, and others were to an auction yard near home.

During the winter of 1948 or 1949 we had six feet of snow. It has never snowed that much before so nobody had a wagon or buggy made for snow. We couldn't feed the cattle and they couldn't find grass to eat or get water to drink. That winter we lost several head of cattle but no chickens or turkeys because they were in a building where I could feed and water them. Six weeks passed before we could go to town. During that time our son Louis, became very ill and I thought he would die. He cried day and night and had a very high fever. There was nothing we could do. We had no telephone and even if we had the doctor could not have come out to the ranch and we could not get to town because of the snow. I stayed up with him every night and all day. This nightmare continued for five days and nights. One night I thought he was no longer living. On the sixth day his fever broke, and he began to slowly recover. Once again I was thankful to God.

Because some of the cattle at the ranch belonged to Dad, he would come out to the ranch at branding and roundup time. He and Mother were ranchers and enjoyed staying and working at the ranch. I often wondered if they ever regretted selling us the ranch and moving to town.

About once a month in the summer they would come out and bring a bag of ice. We would make homemade ice cream with real eggs and thick cream. When Mother had the mixture ready and in the ice cream mixer, we would put the ice in the ice cream maker and sprinkle it with salt. Then we start turning the handle until it was ready to eat. It was <u>soooo</u> good compared to what you would buy from a store in town.

They also enjoyed playing cowboy and cowgirl with Louis and Hazel. We still had our pet horse, Herbie, and our two children always enjoyed riding and playing with him. But when

Grandpa and Grandma came out from town, Herbie was really busy playing with the whole family. Herbie was part of the family along with our dogs Scamper and Big Black Joe. One time Louis and Hazel were missing for some time. I looked all over and called them. I started to worry because it wasn't like them to wander too far from home. Where could they have gone, and where are our dogs? Finally I found them down in the creek, which was really a big mud hole. When I saw them they were covered with mud from head to toe. They were with Big Black Joe, so I felt much better about the situation because I knew he was taking care of them. He was a big black dog and only someone in the family could get close to him. He would take care and protect the children with his life. Scamper was a little dog and would play and run with anybody but I think he liked our Hazel the best. She sometimes would dress him up in doll clothes or cover him up and put him to bed to sleep. Of course when she was three feet away he was up and at her heels.

For Louis' birthday his grandpa gave him a neat little lariat, which became part of his life.

One day he was in a tree with his lariat. One end was tied to the tree limb. He fell out of the tree and the other end caught around his foot. There he was hanging from the tree upside down. Hazel came running in the house yelling, "Mama Mama" Louis is hanging!! I was frantic with worry. I dropped what I was doing and flew outside. When I found him I had a hard time getting him down because he was about eight feet from the ground. Using a ladder I was able to get him down and everything went back to normal, just another day with two very active children. Big black Joe couldn't help him; all he could do was bark and he did his share of barking. Something was always going on with those two on the ranch miles from town.

When Hazel was four years old Fred was born, and two years later I gave birth to Inez.

Chapter"19"

Bob's parents had friends in the state of Wisconsin. He told them about all the deer and antelope we had on the ranch. Two of them wrote letters to us asking if they could come to the ranch and hunt. Bob and I talked about that for a week because it was something new to us. We didn't know what was involved. We knew the hunting season was open the last two weeks in September and the first two weeks in October. We decided that we would give it a try and let two hunters in the first year.

We wrote two of them a letter and informed them what we would charge. They could sleep in our log house because they would leave early in the morning to hunt, and that would not disturb our children. I told them that I would lay out the breakfast food for them which consisted of various kinds of cold cereal, milk and sugar. I would also have the coffee pot full of water with coffee grounds available. All they had to do was turn on the stove and brew it. They would furnish their own lunch but I would make them a big supper. Supper would be potatoes and gravy, beef, pork or chicken, a vegetable and a salad. Dessert was always pie. In the morning Bob would take them out and show them the area where they could hunt, and he would stay with them. We didn't know them but we did know that city men like to shoot and some didn't know the difference between a cow and a deer or antelope. They were also warned there would be no liquor as guns and liquor do not mix. Some hunters would go to town in the evening to drink and talk about their hunt that day and also to buy sandwich material for the next day. The hunters accepted our proposal and arrived with a large freezer chest with dry ice in which to put their deer and antelope meat. It was also used to keep their lunch from spoiling. The first year was a great success and we learned quite a bit from hosting just two hunters. They each shot a deer and an antelope and made plans to come back the following year.

When they returned to their homes in Wisconsin they told their friends all about their hunting experience. For the next ten or fifteen years we had between five and fourteen hunters every week for the entire four week hunting season. One week we had forty hunters, but that was too many. I said no more of that. One hunter went to town and bought a dishwasher and gave it to me as a gift. That was a big help for him and me because prior to that he would help me wash and dry the dishes after supper. We always knew who was coming so we were ready. I tried to have pies, meat and everything I needed before they arrived. Some slept in the log house, some in back of their truck, and some under a tree or in the barn. They all arrived with a sleeping bag and everything they needed.

They were a happy group of men. Every night there was a party after supper. They laughed, played jokes on each other, told stories and all without liquor. The one story they always told was about the hunter that came every year. One year as he got out of his truck, he saw little Inez, about two years old at the time. He started to pick her up for a big hug and Big Black Joe clamped his teeth around his wrist and wouldn't let him go. There he was with that little girl about twelve inches off the ground and that big dog looking him straight into his eyes. He hollered for me and with that voice I knew somebody was in trouble.

I dropped what I was doing, ran out into the yard and rescued him. He had deep teeth marks but shed no blood.

One day two hunters shot a large deer down in a valley where a pickup truck could not go. They went back to the ranch to get a horse. One of the guys said he could ride so he got a horse and put a saddle and bridle on him. He climbed on and the horse promptly bucked him off. He said that only happens once and then the horse settles down. He got back on the horse and again the horse bucked him off. Then he said, Watch This! He won't buck me off again. He took the reins and started walking the horse down to where the deer lay. That was a story that was retold many times.

Another time two boys came with their dad's. While the men were out hunting deer the boys were shooting prairie dogs. After some time they started back to the house and saw two deer near the house. They ran to the house to see if a hunter was there. When they got there the only hunter from Illinois had just arrived with clothes on that looked like he just came home from church. The boys told him about the deer. He grabbed his gun, ran out behind the house, and shot his deer for the season.

Another story they tell was about the evening we had watermelon. I was sitting on top of the chicken coop which was about five feet high. I stepped on a block, climbed on top, and started eating watermelon. I spit the seeds at the chickens and watched them fight over them. If one chicken got two seeds I would yell at it for not sharing.

One hunter who came to the ranch to hunt for several years was diagnosed with cancer. It was a fast growing cancer and his physicians were not certain how long he would live. At hunting season he told his twenty seven year old son, "I want to go hunting at the ranch once more." They agreed on a date and came to the ranch. They saw a nice big deer, but he was too weak to lift his gun so his son held it up while his dad sighted, pulled the trigger and shot his last deer. They stayed at the ranch one more day joking and laughing with the group. They left for home the next day. A day after his arrival at home he died. I'm sure he died the happiest hunter we had that year.

Chapter"20"

When it was time for Louis to start his first year of school he went to live with his grandma, Bob's mother because she was a teacher in a town about seventy miles from our ranch.

When Hazel started school we asked the State of Wyoming if they would give us a teacher to teach our two children at our ranch. They sent us a very nice lady who brought her own small travel trailer to live in. She taught Louis and Hazel in the old log house for one year. She was a very good teacher as well as a good friend. At Christmas time she had our two children put on a Christmas program. We invited all the ranchers in the area to the program. It was a very good delightful program and was the talk among the ranchers for years. After the program I had them all over to our house for a party and Christmas goodies. The evening was so special that when people in town heard about it they wished they could have attended.

The next year we leased the ranch to someone for three years so Bob could go back to school and get his degree in vocational agriculture and elementary education. He wanted a degree so he could teach our children at the ranch and also to be a better rancher. We moved to Laramie and bought a house close to the University of Wyoming. While Bob was in school I started babysitting other people's children for extra income. When he received his degree we couldn't return to the ranch because it was still under lease for one more year. We moved to Gillette, and Bob worked at the State of Wyoming Experimental Station. There he worked with wool, cattle, plants, and other things related to ranching and to his degree. While in Gillette Louis and Hazel went to school and I stayed home with Fred and baby Inez. We lived in a one bedroom apartment with a stove that didn't have an oven. Rental apartments or homes were not available at any price because the coal and oil industries were just getting started in that area. We considered ourselves lucky to get the apartment we had. We moved in as the other tenant was moving out. We were in Gillette for only one year and that was about all we could manage in that one bedroom apartment. Bob enjoyed his work but our apartment was not much more than a hole to crawl into with four children.

Chapter "21"

The lease was up on our ranch and we happily returned to life on the ranch. That summer Bob went back to school for three months to get his teaching certificate. He decided to build a schoolhouse on the ranch. It was made with regular lumber and had a stove in the middle for heat in the winter. The children had regular school desks and a blackboard just like a school in town. Bob started teaching Louis, Hazel, and Fred on the ranch. During school hours our children called Bob Mister or Sir. He wore a suit and tie and the children wore good school clothes.

While Bob taught the three older children I took care of Inez and did the ranch work. I had to take care of the cattle, feed them cattle cubes and hay in the winter and break the ice in the water tank. I also had to make sure the water pumps and the windmills were working. I repaired fences and kept the cattle where they belonged. I took Inez with me if I used the truck and when I had to go by horseback she would sit in front of me. I think she enjoyed riding horseback with me best of all. One time I used the truck and got stuck in the mud. I walked home with Inez on my back. When I got home Inez's legs were asleep and she couldn't stand up for a while. That was the first time that happened to her and she was afraid that she would never stand or walk again. A few minutes later she was her wild self again. My friends asked me if I wouldn't have liked teaching the children instead of doing the ranch work. I answered NO. The cattle don't talk back or ask a lot of foolish questions like the children do, plus, I enjoy being outside and interacting with animals.

On one of my trips checking the cattle I noticed a steer didn't act normally. The next day Bob told me to bring that steer in and take it to the veterinarian. It snowed all day and night. I rode my horse looking for the steer. The sun reflected off the snow and burned my lips. Two months passed before they began to heal. Bob thought it was cancer. I found the steer, brought him home, loaded him onto the truck and took him to the veterinarian. The veterinarian gave him a shot of something and said to keep him in the corral a couple days with enough food and water. In a few days he was well.

Several years later Bob and I realized that my work with the cattle was consuming most of my time and was detrimental to Inez. She was three and about to celebrate her fourth birthday when Bob and I decided that she could start kindergarten. When we told her, she was so excited that she didn't sleep all night. She was going to school with her brothers and older sister.

Bob wasn't prepared for this change. She was to young and had a short attention span. Bob complained saying he had a degree and teaching certificate in elementary education not babysitting. Three days later she began to settle down and learned to follow the rules. When quiet returned to the classroom Bob commenced to teach again. When the year had ended Inez could count and write her numbers from one to twenty. She knew all the basic colors and could say or sing most of the alphabet. Every year our children were tested by the Wyoming school district. Each year they scored average or higher than the other students in that district. The last year Bob taught at the ranch, Louis ranked above all the other students in that district. Both Bob and Louis, teacher and student were ecstatic, intoxicated with job for a months.

Chapter "22"

Inez was too young yet but the other three children learned to ride horseback on Herbie. He was a playmate to them as he was to me. At Christmas the children got a big red fire truck with a bell on it from Santa. One day I heard the fire truck bell tingling and tingling and wondered why it never stopped. I was sure they couldn't pedal it that long. I looked out and saw they had a rope tied from the fire truck to the saddle on Herbie. Louis was riding Herbie and the children were taking turns riding in the fire truck and ringing the bell.

Herbie was not only a pet but a life saver. One winter day Bob had to go out in the pasture to tend to the cattle. He was on Herbie, and as he left it started to snow. Before he was finished with his work the snow turned into a blizzard, so fierce that he couldn't see five feet in front of him. He turned Herbie towards home but Herbie wanted to go in a different direction. After several attempts he told Herbie, let's go home, to the barn. A little while later he realized Herbie was changing directions but let him go. Herbie kept walking and about two hours later he stopped in front of the barn with my very cold and surprised husband.

Herbie was a real joy to all of us. He was a good work horse and a good friend. One day I noticed that he wasn't acting normal and I wondered if he was getting too old. I talked to Bob about it and he agreed that Herbie might be nearing the end of his life. Bob decided he would take him to the veterinarian the next day and have him checked. When he returned he told me Herbie was old and also had cancer from which he would suffer until he died. He offered to give him an injection to put him to sleep or we could do as other ranchers do, just take him out in the pasture and shoot him. Bob took him a long way out on the range and shot him with his three fifty seven revolver. Good old Herbie is now in horse heaven.

Chapter "23"

One day while Bob was teaching our children, I went out in the pasture to round up and bring in some cattle to be treated for grubs. The female grubs lay eggs on the cow's leg hair. As it hatches it digs or bores into the cow and travels up though the animal to the back. As it emerges, it leaves an infested sore. That sore could cause the cow to lose weight or die. On my way back to the ranch my horse stepped in a hole, and I flew over his head and landed on my back. My horse trying not to fall, stepped on my leg and my hand. I knew my hand would swell up so I took my wedding ring off. I had no pocket so I put it in my mouth. I got back on my horse and took the cattle home. Once I was at home I spit the ring out and put it in my jewelry box. Then Hazel and I got in the trusty old truck, started the engine, rammed it in gear and floored it. We had to get to town **to** have my hand and leg x-rayed. By this time I had terrible pain in both my hand and leg. At the first auto gate I tried to lift my leg to slow down but it wouldn't move. I finally got the truck stopped and said to Hazel, "You have to drive." She was only twelve but ranch and farm children learn to drive very early in life. It is more out of necessity than for enjoyment.

The doctor concluded there were no broken bones in my leg but that I had a smashed hand which he could not provide any treatment for. He sent me home and instructed me to stay off my feet and not use my hand for a several weeks. I was very careful for a week or until it stopped hurting so bad, and then it was back to work. I still had ranch work to do and Bob had to teach every day or the government would close our school.

When it was time for the cows to have their calves our days and nights ran together. The first part of March we would bring all the cows in from the winter pasture to a pasture near the ranch buildings. Then we would separate the cows with big bags from those with little or no bags. Those with little or no bags were returned to the open pasture. Every day I would ride out and check the cows. When their bags were big and heavy I would bring them to a trap near the house. Then the long hours started. I would check them every three or four hours during the day to see if they were having their babies. At night Bob and I would take turns checking them and as Louie and Hazel got older they too took turns at night. If we saw a cow looking for a place to hide we would watch her to see if she was having a natural birth or if she was having a problem. Ninety five percent of our cows had no problem but if we saw a cow ringing her tail, stomping around, and sometimes kicking at her belly, we would bring her in the barn to watch her. If she didn't have her baby in about twenty or thirty minutes after her water broke, I would put my arm in the birth canal all the way to my shoulder to find out what the problem was. If the calf had its front legs pointing out, all I had to do was grab the legs and pull when the cow had a contraction. That only occurred when the calf was too large for a normal birth. If I could not feel the legs I would have to try and turn the calf around and get it in the right position. By that time the cow was too weak to push and I was too tired to pull so I would have to wake Bob to come help. Every week we had about one or two cows that needed our help. Bob was still teaching our children in the school house so during the day I had to do it all the best I could.

Chapter "24"

It was time for Louis and Hazel to start high school. My Dad and Mother eagerly agreed to move back to the ranch and we moved to Lusk Wyoming, about sixty miles from the ranch. Bob taught sixth grade and Louis and Hazel went to high school there. Fred and Inez went to the same school where Bob taught. The school was only two blocks from the house we rented. Bob was in Lusk only one year because my Dad died and we had to return to the ranch. My Mother returned to Douglas and lived in the house they owned.

That same year Bob's mother and dad were killed by a train at a railroad crossing in Douglas. They owned and lived on a ranch that was only five miles from town. Their ranch was smaller than our ranch and we pondered over the idea to buy it from their estate. There were good reasons. One big reason was, our children could go to school in Douglas. They could get on a school bus with just a short walk from the ranch house to the road and be in school in fifteen minutes. We also concluded that it would be a lot more work for Bob and me each living and working on separate ranches. Our two boys, Louis and Fred, were getting older and would be a big help to me after school. After weighing our options we bought the ranch from the estate and the children and I moved to that ranch. The ranch house was old and small but it was much larger than the little apartment we had in Gillette so we didn't complain.

It was a sheep ranch with sheep so we bought the sheep also. I took care of the sheep on that ranch and Bob took care of the cattle on the big ranch. At lambing time I had my hands full with taking care of the children, our home and the sheep. At the end of lambing I had seven orphan lambs that the children helped me bottle feed and take care of until they could survive on their own. Every Friday after school we returned to the big ranch where Bob was living and working. Then we went back to Douglas Sunday evening so the children could go to school on Monday. When we went to the big ranch I drove our old pickup truck that had only a bench seat and no seat belts. I put Louis and Hazel in the back with the lamb milk and bottles. Then I handed Louis and Hazel each two lambs to hold all the way to the big ranch. In the front seat Fred held two lambs and Inez held her little pet lamb.

My mother's health deteriorated and I began to stay with her in town as much as I could. I also had to take care of our children and work with the sheep on the small ranch. This routine continued for five years. The last three years Mother resided in the nursing home or was hospitalized. When she was in the nursing home and hospital I visited her daily and made sure she ate her food. The children and I stayed at the little ranch until all our children graduated from high school.

Every morning after I put the children on the school bus I would find the sheep somewhere in the pasture and make sure they had water and were doing well. There were many predators that loved to kill and eat our sheep. My boys trapped and shot as many as they could but more still came.

One winter morning I loaded the truck with hay and drove it to the water well. The sheep were always there in the winter because that is where I fed them and that is where they drank their water. It was extremely cold that morning and the water pump was not working because it was frozen. I tried to turn the wheel with my gloved hand. As it started to turn, my thumb with the glove on became entangled in the wheel. The pain was almost unbearable and it started to bleed profusely. I jumped in the truck and raced down the road to town and to the hospital. As I stepped inside the hospital door I fainted. I woke up in the operating room with an IV in my arm. When I asked what it was for, I was informed it was medicine to kill the pain. The nurse cut my glove off and threw it in the trash can. The doctor washed my hand, and I overheard him say, "The end of her thumb is missing. Check the glove to see if it's in there." The nurse went to the trash can and retrieved the glove. After washing it off she looked inside and there was the end of my thumb. The doctor carefully cleaned the end of my thumb and attached it to the remaining part of my thumb. He advised that I stay in the hospital until I recovered from the pain medicine. I told him I had work to do at the ranch and my children would be home from school soon. He replied, with the pain medicine I gave you to alleviate some of the pain, you shouldn't drive. "I answered, I can't walk either." As I started to leave, he admonished me to drive slowly and carefully. He was a western cowboy doctor and understood ranchers. I left the hospital and drove back to the ranch. Of course, the water pump did not fix itself while I was gone, so I stopped at the shop and picked up some big tools. With my left hand I was able to get the pump working. My sheep were happy to get a drink of water. I unloaded some hay for them and went home. I was exhausted and thought about sitting down and having a cup of something to drink or eat but didn't know what I wanted so I settled for a drink of water. Remembering what my Dad called coffee convinced me to never drink coffee, and I never drank liquor, so water was my only option.

One winter night it snowed so much that we couldn't get out of the house door. We had a fire in our potbellied stove for heat but somehow we had to get out of the house to get wood for our stove and check on the sheep. Sheep won't try to get out of the snow, they will just lie there and die. Louis climbed out the window, found a shovel and shoveled the snow away from the front door so we could all get out. The children met the bus to go to school, and I went to check on the sheep. True to their nature most of them were just lying in the snow waiting to die. I kicked and shoved them until they were all moving. We didn't lose a single sheep in that snow storm. At the big ranch, Bob had lots of snow but no major problems. The only problem he had was being alone and without me and our children during the week.

Chapter "25"

When Louis finished high school he joined the Navy and was first stationed in California and later in Texas. Hazel finished high school one year after Louis and started college to become a nurse. Fred and Inez remained with me and were a big help taking care of the sheep, fixing fences, checking the windmills and repairing the corral. My Mother passed away and that left me with more time to work on the small ranch and tend to the sheep. We had sheep with a good grade of wool which sold for a good price. When our sheep got old and lost their teeth we would sell them on the market for meat or as it is called: "counter canners."

Louis married while still in the Navy. After he was discharged he and his wife came home. We decided to hire both him and his wife to work on the big ranch, Enabling Bob to live and work with me on the small ranch. Bob and I plus all four of our children, owned cattle on the big ranch so to hire Louis was the only way to alleviate the problem of who would be responsible for taking care of the cows. Eventually the children sold their cattle or took them to establish their own homes.

Chapter "26"

The house we lived in on the small ranch was very small and old. The time came when we had to decide whether to repair it, enlarge it or build a new one. We discovered the cost to repair was more than the house was worth so we decided to build a new one. Bob worked every day with the contractor trying to save some money on the project.

After the house was completed Bob was not feeling well. We attributed it to the many long days of hard work on our new house and the ranch work he had done throughout his life. We bought an Airstream travel trailer, joined the Airstream club and began travelling. By this time Fred was old enough to take care of the small ranch and Inez got married and moved from the ranch. That left us free to finally enjoy life. When it turned cold we went to Arizona for the winter. In the spring we returned to the ranch but Bob continued to feel sick. He went to the doctor and was informed that he was suffering from emphysema, an incurable pulmonary disease. He continued to work on both ranches but we managed to take some pleasure trips and spend our winters in Arizona. In a few years he periodically needed oxygen. Eventually he needed to carry an oxygen tank with him. His health declined to the point where I had to hook up the Airstream to the car and do all the driving when we travelled. He enjoyed going to the Airstream rallies so we continued to do that. When he was using oxygen twenty-four seven and getting weaker, I had to carry his oxygen tank. I didn't mind that. After all, he was my husband for forty two years and I loved him. We were a team. This was our life for ten years. Louis was taking care of the big ranch, and Fred was taking care of the small ranch. Bob was hospitalized his last twenty five days and I stayed with him. He was a good husband and father to our children. He was well liked and respected by his fellow ranchers and everybody in towns and cities in the State of Wyoming. He was trust worthy, educated, of good character, and belonged to several professional organizations in Wyoming. I can't say enough good things about him because he was everything to me.

Chapter "27"

I lived at the small ranch and supervised the work on both ranches. I helped the boys when needed. I continued going to the Airstream Rallies. Hooking up and driving was no problem because I had been doing it for many years. I owned a Park Model Trailer in Arizona so when winter came, I went to Arizona and lived in it.

I stayed busy all the time. In addition to the ranch work I was president of the county homemakers club and a member of Wyoming State Quealy club for thirty eight years.

The following summer there was a big International Airstream Rally in Boise Idaho. I had no reason not to go so I hooked up the Airstream and drove to Boise. Over four thousand Airstream Travel Trailers and Motorhomes all parked in straight rows. The parkers were gracious, friendly and efficient. They offered to help me park, but I told them I knew how to do it. When I finished they were amazed at my ability to park a travel trailer.

After I unhooked it and connected to water and electricity, I went to the main auditorium. In a side room they had set up tables to advertise the Airstream rally programs and club information. Inside the Airstream club there are sub clubs such as singles clubs, bowling clubs, golf clubs, etc.

I met some friends there that I knew from other Airstream rallies that I had attended. One of the ladies was single and asked me to help her set up a table for single men and woman who owned an Airstream and wanted to meet other singles. I told her I would help her but I was not ready to meet a man. When we finished setting up the tables and were ready to leave, a very handsome man came by and asked us if we could square dance because every night there was square dancing at the rally. We said, we did not square dance and he moved on. My friend said, "I want him, he is so good looking." I told her she could have him as I was still grieving over the loss of my husband and was not ready for a relationship with any man handsome or not.

The Airstream unit of which I was a member, was hosting a Rally the following month in my home town. The person in charge of the rally asked me to help set up the table and hand out flyers the next day promoting the Rally. The next day as I was working at the table the same good looking man came by. I asked him if he was coming to my rally and handed him a flyer. He said he was not attending because he had to be in Washington DC at the time of the rally. I proceeded to ask him if he found a square dance partner. He said no and had walked away. We ran into each other once after a program but we didn't speak or even acknowledge one another. What I did notice was that he always looked so neat, clean, respectable and always wore half a smile.

When the rally was over, I hooked up my Airstream and went back to the ranch in Douglas. I stayed busy on both ranches and assisted in getting things ready for our Airstream Rally in town. For some unknown reason the man I had casually met at the rally in Boise, kept coming into my mind.. I wasn't ready for a man and I didn't even know his name. I was certain I'd never see him again so I told myself, to get him out of my mind.

On the second day of our Rally in my home town, there he was, sitting in the second row attending one of our programs. Why was he here? Did he come because I invited him and gave him a flyer? Certainly he didn't come to see me. He didn't know me and why wasn't he in Washington, DC as he said. Throughout the rally he didn't talk to me or even look at me. My friends told me to speak to him. He was probably attending because I had invited him. On the last evening we had a dinner for all the attendees. Because I had mentioned him to my friends earlier they made certain I was seated next to him. I could not believe it. He spoke to the people across the table and to the people on his left but never even looked or said anything to me seated on his right. I didn't say anything to him either, maybe I was afraid, being single and at my age a person has different feeling. What could or should I say? When the dinner was over and they started to take up the tables, I went up to him and asked, "Did you have a good time at our Rally?" He looked at me for a few seconds then said, Yes, it's one of the best rallies I ever attended and you are the one that invited me. I was looking for you. I thought to myself, that he is really full of it. Later he told me that he forgot what I looked like and he had no intention of coming to this rally. He had stayed in the Boise area square dancing and sightseeing longer than he intended. He was now on his way to Washington, DC and planned to stay overnight in a campground here in Douglas. When he pulled off the road he saw a lot of Airstreams and then he remembered what a lady had told him at the Boise rally.

We talked for a while about the rally. He said he really enjoyed it because it was so different from any rally he had ever attended. We had horses, cowboys, shooting, sheep shearing, a mock hanging and everything wild west. I told him it was all put on for city people and tourist. A real ranch today was much different and that I owned a ranch. I asked him if he would like to see a real live working ranch. Being the inquisitive person he was, he very excitedly said, Yes. I don't know why I was running my mouth to a man I had met only about half an hour before. What will I do now? I really trapped myself. So, I told him I was leaving the rally the next morning to go to my ranch and he could follow me if he desired. He did!

When we arrived at the ranch I introduced him to my youngest son Fred, and his wife, and showed him the ranch house. He liked it and said it was surly different from houses he lived in or visited. There was a saddle, a saddle blanket and a halter on the railing as we entered. Inside the house there was a deer head with antlers and an antelope head with horns and horns six feet long from a Texas Long Horned Bull. There was also an eight foot long Rattle Snake skin. By the time I finished showing him around the ranch buildings and the corral it was time to eat dinner. My son's wife had the meal ready for us. As we sat down Don noticed that each of us at the table had a steak on our plate. The rest of the meal was in the middle of the table. Don looked at his steak and remarked that it was more meat than he had eaten in five years. He explained that he didn't want to appear ungrateful but he would try to eat two square inches if I would cut that much off the steak. I wondered if that was why he is so thin. Then he told us that he didn't eat much red meat. My son informed him that on the ranch half raw red meat was the main course and if we were still hungry after that we finished up with potatoes. He and my son related quite well. They talked and joked about everything. After dinner we walked around the ranch buildings and he asked about the animals and seemed genuinely interested in ranching.

He wanted to leave the next morning but I invited him to stay and see the big ranch. At that time he did not know I owned two. He consented to stay another day. We drove my pickup truck fifty miles to the big ranch. He couldn't believe we lived so far from town and only about ten miles were paved. He was surprise to see how rough the ranch roads were, plus he had never seen an auto gate. Everything appeared to be new to him and he tried to see it all. He had a thousand questions. He was like a kid.

When we arrived at the ranch I introduced him to my oldest son, Louis. After we talked I asked Louis if he would take us for a ride in the truck and show Don the ranch.

Louis took us to the worst and roughest part of the ranch. At times I thought we would tip over or fall in a deep ditch. Finally, I asked Louis to stop the truck and let me out. He stopped, I got out. Louis said they would be back in a little while to pick me up. He wanted to show Don some more of the ranch. Fifteen minutes later he came back, and Don was all smiles. He really enjoyed the ride and was fascinated by everything he saw. A few days later, Louis told me that he was trying to scare Don so he would never come back because Don was from the city and was not like us. Louis did not want me to become involved with him.

None the less we had a good time together for those two days. We talked about so many things, places he worked and lived, and the kind of work he did. He was a very interesting man. He also asked questions about me. We could have talked longer but he said that he had to leave, considering that he was expected to be in Washington, DC a week before.

The next day Don hooked up his Airstream and left.

I missed him. What was wrong with me? I needed to slow down and think. I wondered if I'd ever see him again. He promised to write. He seemed to be honest and a man true to his word.

Chapter"28"

Two weeks later I received a letter from him. He finished his business in Washington, DC, spent time with his children and was now back in the Florida Keys. He had a good trip but could not get me out of his mind. He repeated how much he enjoyed meeting me and thanked me for showing him the ranches. Then he said he hoped we could get together again sometime, somewhere. I don't know why but I also hoped we could get together again.

He lives in his Airstream and has not yet looked for a job. He wrote that jobs were not readily available until the tourists arrive in November.

We exchanged letters for several months. In October I told him I was preparing to go to Arizona for the winter. I gave him my address and phone number in Arizona and suggested he call me. In his next letter he wrote that he had nothing planned for the winter and I was to let him know what day I planned to be in Arizona. He could bring his Airstream and stay in the same Park if there was a space for him.

A few days after I arrived in Arizona, he came arriving in the Park with his Airstream. I was really glad to see him, but I'm still not sure why. Was I ready for a relationship? He was a really nice guy, and I would have someone to be with everyday I'm here at the Park. Maybe I could take lessons and learn to square dance.

He called himself a health nut. He exercised every morning before he did anything. It made him feel better and got him off to a good start for the day. Some mornings he would come over to my trailer after breakfast, and we would do stretching exercises. He did his for forty five minutes and I would last thirty minutes and quit. Following our exercises we would walk for two miles and talk. When we returned home he would read from his Bible and preach to me a little. Several months later he started to say things like, "you should get saved." I went to church once in a while before I met Don, but our preacher never said anything about being saved. Don told me that he was a Christian and since he was saved he belonged to a Baptist church and helped wherever he was needed. Every Sunday since coming to Arizona he would take me to church. I enjoyed hearing him sing. He knew all the songs. A few months later he referred me to verses in the Bible that say you must be saved to go to heaven. He showed me: Rom 6:23, Rom 10:9 - 10 and a few other verses. Shortly after that I asked Jesus to forgive me for all my sins because He is the only person who died on the cross for all my sins. I asked Him to come into my heart and take control of my life. I will always trust him as my Savior. A week later I was baptized by emersion the way Jesus was in the Jordan River.

We stayed busy shopping or looking at things in stores and rode our bicycles all over the park and town. I started taking square dance lessons, and we became very involved in park activities. It was early February when we came home from church that Don took my hand and asked me to sit down. He said that he has been praying and asking God for a wife for almost a year. Then he said; "I love you, and I believe you are the lady God wants me to marry. Will you marry me?" I was not too surprised because I loved him too. I wanted to accept his proposal but first I had to talk to my children. That night I called and spoke to all four of my children. Inez said, if it would make you happy, then do it. The other three were one hundred percent against it. All night I thought and prayed about it. I felt happy, content and satisfied being with him and I trusted him. Did I need to live according to the wishes and desires of my children? Wasn't my life my own business? I couldn't live with or for my children. They were all adults and on their own.

When Don arrived at my door the next morning, I raised my voice and said "<u>YES! I'll marry you</u>". We hugged and kissed for what seemed like an hour. We talked about the details of the wedding, and I asked him if we could wait a few weeks and get married on my birthday, February twenty fifth. He agreed to the plan and we were married on my birthday in Mesa Arizona. February is now a very special month for me. I was saved, baptized and married Don in the month of February. What a memorable and joyful month that was and continues to be. Every time I think back on that special February, I say, "Thank you Jesus."

Chapter "29"

I remember the day after he arrived in Arizona for the first time. I wanted to invite him over for dinner but I wasn't sure what to prepare for him. I remember his saying at the ranch that he didn't eat much red meat. Ranch people have meat at every meal. For breakfast we had bacon, eggs and toasted white bread with real butter. For dinner and supper we had some kind of red meat with potatoes, gravy, and a vegetable followed by dessert. When I told him what we normally ate he said that he didn't eat like that. For breakfast he ate hot cereal four times a week and cold cereal three times with raw honey for sweetener. The hot cereal was steel cut oats, oat bran, oat meal or ten grain cereal. Cold cereal was cheerios, bran flakes or shredded wheat. He also put ground flax seed over all of his cereal and used skim milk. He liked fruits and vegetables and his meat preferences were fish or turkey breast. He said he had been eating like that since he began medical research at the National Institutions of Health. When he left his White

House job he was forty five pounds overweight and just didn't feel normal. After he adopted a new regimen of eating and exercising, he lost the excess weight and felt great ever since.

I knew I was overweight. When Bob was ill he had to eat small meals often, and I would eat a little with him. I asked Don if he would work with me and help me lose weight. He consented. We cooked, ate and exercised together. Within six months I had lost all of my excess weight and all my aches and pains that I was experiencing.

Don has been making breakfast for us every day since we started our new life together. He also enjoys baking. When he looks at a recipe, he hates that many of the ingredients are unhealthy so he alters them. He has many recipes that are his own such as his recipe for bread. He makes our bread the old fashion way using twelve different kinds of flour and raw honey instead of sugar. If a recipe calls for eggs, he will use ground flax seed with a little water or an egg substitute from a health food store or egg whites only. He has not eaten an egg yolk for forty years because of the cholesterol. He is also very careful about saturated fat that produces cholesterol. He prefers fat free foods or ingredients in his cooking and always includes some high fiber. A food with high fiber will fill your stomach more quickly and stays with you longer. White flour, white rice and white sugar are forbidden. The nutrients are bleached out, and then vitamins are added back in to give it some nutritional value. It's also very important to know family histories and family genes.

I once cooked him a special dinner with a baked turkey breast, a baked sweet potato topped with cinnamon and margarine and peas for a vegetable. For dessert we had a pistachio pudding with marshmallows, and fat free cream. He thanked me and admitted it was the best dinner he had eaten in years, especially, since he didn't have to shop, cook it and eat alone. After that we cooked together, had loads of fun and enjoyed each other's company.

Chapter "30"

Every morning when we walked Don would comment on the pollution. One morning we saw a couple wearing masks as they walked. Don mentioned that we should either buy masks or walk later in the day. We started walking later in the day but it was almost too hot to walk and enjoy it. Being as health conscious as he is, he suggested that we spend the next winter in a different area. He lived in the Florida Keys for a few years and told me the air is always clean because it comes off the ocean. The Florida Keys are a connection of islands and no matter which island you live on you always have fresh clean air to breathe. I thought to myself; he is a good salesman. He should work for the Florida Chamber of Commerce. I suggested that we talk about it later. I owned my Park Model Trailer in Arizona and didn't want to sell it plus I had so many friends there. Don made friends easily and went to a high level square dance club twice a week. I started square dance lesson and attended the class twice a week with Don as my helper/partner or in square dance terms, angel. I finished the basic and mainstream level and most of the plus level when it was time to go back to Wyoming and my ranch. We square danced in Casper once a week where I learned the rest of the plus level. We danced once in Gillette and twice in Cheyenne at special dances. We enjoyed Cheyenne the most. The square dance building was a very old rail road building with a good hard wood floor. It was so old and beautiful that it was on the government register for historical buildings.

In Cheyenne and a few other places you were allowed to spend the night in your RV next to the building. That was always a big plus for us because after square dancing for three hours or more we didn't feel like driving some distance to a campground.

When we danced with a square dance caller or round dance cuer for the first time, I would have them sign their name on a piece of paper. Then I would transfer it to my white skirt and embroider it. Each caller or curer had a different color. When I stopped dancing at age eighty five years old I had two hundred and sixty eight signatures embroidered on my skirt.

Chapter "31"

All that summer and ensuing summers we stayed busy at the ranch. Don was so inquisitive about his new life that he had a thousand questions every day. He assisted at branding time. At first he was a little in the way of progress but finally he found a job he could do and he enjoyed doing it. While the calf was being branded he would do the inoculation. We laughed at him because he treated the calf as if it were a person, sometimes he even talked to it.

Two days before branding the boys rounded up all the cattle. The cattle usually congregate in groups of fifty to seventy five. The morning of the branding the cows are separated from their calves. The wives of my two sons put the calves in the chute and the boys did the branding. Because all four children and I owned cattle, I had to tell the boys which branding iron to use and I did the inventory or accounting. We each had our own registered brand. The ear tag on the calf is the same as its mother and is given to him or her at birth. When a calf had its brand and its inoculation it was turned out to be with its mother who was waiting for it. The calf would be hungry and the mother had a full bag. Branding was a noisy activity because the mother was calling her baby and the calf was being hurt by the branding iron.

Every summer Don and I would help brand the cattle at the big ranch. Then we would go to the little ranch to brand the sheep after they were sheared. We also helped docking the lambs.(cutting the tails off.) It takes a long time for the lamb and the mother sheep to get back together. It appears that they really don't care. Sheep are peculiar animals.

Chapter "32"

When there was nothing for Don and me to do at the ranch we started planning trips. We decided that each summer after branding was finished we would go someplace. The following pages contain the trips we went on.

There is so much to see in Wyoming that we didn't know where to start. Our first summer trip was on the recommendation of an Airstream friend that knew where there were some very old prehistoric pictographs in a cave. He advised us to wear good walking shoes because we could only drive within a few miles of the place. It was a long rough walk but it was worth every step. They were beautiful and something we will never forget. We were informed that very few people know about them. He instructed us not to tell anybody the location. He didn't want vandals or treasure hunters to come in and destroy the place. It was on private property and we had to ask permission to go on it just as the hunters had to do during hunting season.

On this trip we also went to the Medicine

Wheel in the Bighorn National Forest. To the Native Americans from years ago it had religious, astronomical and calendrical significance. It is also known as the sacred hoop. It embodies the four directions as well as Father Sky, Mother Earth and Spirit Tree, all of which symbolize dimensions of health and the cycles of life. It was all very interesting.

The second summer we went to see the Oregon Trail Ruts just south of Guernsey. It was used from 1841 to 1869 by emigrants traveling west. The Ruts were cut in a sandstone ridge by wagon wheels, animals, and people. They were between two and six feet deep going across the ridge. One hundred to nine hundred people traveled that route every year. It is hard to comprehend how those people thought or felt. It was a burdensome distressing trip and some died on the way.

For our third summer trip we drove to Independence Rock. The rock is one hundred thirty feet high by nineteen hundred feet long by eight hundred fifty feet wide. It was a place that the emigrants traveling west had to pass before the fourth of July in order to beat the winter snow fall in the mountains. Many of them carved their names in the rock as they passed. Many are still visible today.

For the fourth summer we decided to take a long trip and go to Cody Wyoming to visit the Firearms Museum. Because it was too far for a one day trip, we took our Airstream and stayed in an RV Park. The museum has the most comprehensive collection of fire arms in the world. It also has an amazing collection of artifacts from the early western days. We spent three days in Cody and could have stayed longer, since there is much to see and do in Cody. In the evening we went square dancing with the Cody square dance club. We met some very friendly dancers who lived in Cody and ranchers that lived miles outside of Cody. Square dancers never count miles. They just go because they know that when they get there they will have fun. One rancher we talked with spent the night in a motel. The next day he and his wife would do their monthly shopping and then drive back to their ranch. Liquor is not allowed at the clubs and if someone smokes they do it away from the building.

We left for home after three days but on the way we stopped in Thermopolis Wyoming for a swim in the hot pool. Thermopolis is the home of numerous natural hot springs that are mineral laden and heated by geothermal process. We swam and soaked in hot water for a few hours, and then went down a large hot water slide. All these activities took place in a very large building in town.

The fifth summer was to Utah. Again it was too far for a day trip so we took our Airstream and spent a few days in an RV Park. We drove our truck to an old ghost town a long way off of the highway. When the road ended we had to walk about one mile but it was worth it. We saw old tombstones, foundations from old buildings, old fence post, a rusty old wheelbarrow, all from the Wild West days. Everything was from one hundred to a hundred and fifty years old. We were thinking of all the stories that old town held.

The next day we went to the Arches National Park. It has over two thousand natural stone arches. The largest one resembles a horse shoe. It was all very interesting and stunning. We also had a tour though the Mormon Tabernacle or Temple. We wanted to square dance with the local club but it was not their dance night and we didn't want to spend another day and night.

The sixth summer we made a trip to Idaho. We took our Airstream and made it a four day trip. This time we planned it so we would be there on a square dance night. The first day we went to another ghost town. It was a small town with an old gold mine next to it. The mine was open but we chose not to go in it. We saw tools and old rusty equipment lying around. The buildings in town were falling apart and we wondered what was supporting them. There was also an old cemetery dating back to the late eighteen hundreds with a metal fence around it that was also falling down.

At square dancing that night a dancer told us about an old gold mining machine that was a long distance out in the country. It sounded very interesting. I asked him if he would take us out there. He said he had to work, but he drew a map for us and gave us his telephone number. We drove about forty miles and walked what seemed to be ten more miles up and down hills or small mountains. The trees were tall and thick. Then we saw a steel or iron railroad track that just originated there in the woods. We couldn't see where it came from or where it went. There were trees growing in the center of the track. Some were thirty or forty feet tall. We kept walking, and then we saw a big machine, just sitting there in a big deep ditch or trough about twenty feet wide and six to eight feet deep. It was a small factory with a machine attached to the front to dig down and bring the ground into the machine. Then all the minerals were separated such as, gold, silver, copper, etc. The ground without minerals would be thrown up on each side of the factory. When we saw it, there was a pile of stones about five or six feet high on each side of the ditch for miles and miles. As old as it was, there was very little rust or rot. We walked through the whole factory. There were two big engines and electric wires running all over the factory some with light bulbs hanging down about seven inches. There were long trays, screens, belts and pulleys. We never saw even a picture of anything like that. When we got back to town we asked a few people about it and either they didn't know or they didn't care. I suspected they didn't want their quaint little town overrun with tourists and treasure hunters. I called our square dance friend and asked him about the railroad track. He said during World War Two someone, he didn't know who, removed part of the tracks for the iron tracks to help with the war. It was all very interesting and something we will never forget.

On our way home we stopped once again in Thermopolis for a swim. This time we stayed at a campground which had a hot mineral pool. When we registered we thought it was a little expensive, but then the clerk proceeded to tell us that our site came with breakfast in the pool. The next morning we went to the pool and were glad we did. The pool water was hot and the breakfast was delicious. After breakfast we went for a long walk. Once again we went to town and swam in the big pool and made a trip down the hot water slide. All that hot water is so relaxing. We have enjoyed so many unforgettable experiences that we hope to live many more years. In fact we have had so much fun and excitement in our travels that I am not anxious to get back to the ranch, but the time has come to make that trip.

On our way back to the ranch, standing on the side of the road was a large mountain lion. It was just standing there watching the traffic. In Wyoming there is very little traffic but countless animals of all kinds. Had we slowed down to look, it would have vanished.

Chapter "33"

On a lovely, warm, sunny day in May I finally got Don on a horse again. This time we had our horses walk instead of run. He enjoyed it and we rode in a different direction about once a week all summer long. There was so much I wanted to show him that we could only see from horseback. He could not see enough nor ask enough questions. He enjoyed riding on his horse as long as it didn't run. We took drinking water and a lunch several times and stayed out all day. On one trip Don found an arrow head left by the Indians long ago. On one ride we found some pieces of old pottery from the Indian days. One year we found a piece of a rifle that could have been left by Soldiers, Indians or Settlers. Don also found a lot of beautiful little stones that he wanted to keep. We have a big pile of unusual stones of different sizes and shapes on the little ranch, so I didn't pick up any more. Don filled his pockets with little stones that he thought were pretty. On a big old ranch like mine there is no telling what you might find, and Don was always looking for interesting things. He asked me if I ever found gold on the ranch. My answer was, I never looked.

He got off and on his horse a dozen times to look at something that sparked his curiosity. This went on every summer. He thoroughly enjoyed every day we were home at the ranch. He looked so out of place in his western boots and western hat. You could tell he was a city guy but he was all mine. I really loved him and I knew we had a very happy and exciting life ahead of us. He often said, I wonder what the guys that I once worked with would say if they could see me now. He will never be a cowboy but he enjoyed playing the role. On one trip he took along his revolver. It was a thirty eight special with a one inch barrel. He carried it on his belt. I told him that is not the way cowboys wore their guns and their gun didn't look like his. He said they just don't know what a good gun is. He said, I just want to shoot it and this is a good place to do it. He didn't see anything to shoot on the entire trip so he never carried it again. He claimed he could hit a bulls-eye at twenty five feet anything farther away than that he would really scare them.

I told him the names of plants that my Mother

taught me. One of the times he got off his horse he saw a horned toad. The first one he had ever seen in his life. I informed him that we also had horned lizards on the ranch, but I couldn't find one to show him on this ride. We also saw herds of antelope and in the spring we saw many baby antelope. They are so cute. Sometimes when we were riding on our horses we would see a deer. Antelope stay out all day but deer tend to be out in the evening or at night unless they are awakened from their sleep or hiding place. During the day you rarely see a baby deer because the mother deer hides them really well, and with their spots and light brown color they really blend into their surroundings.

I had many ranch friends. Every weekend about ten of us would get together, visit, eat and play cards. The one that won the most hands was awarded a gift. One day Don won the most and his prize was a nail clipper with a knife blade. He still has it and still uses it. Don liked all my friends, and they liked him. They asked him lots of questions about his life and especially about his White House days. They wanted to know all about President Kennedy and President Johnson.

The men wanted to know about President Johnson's ranch and the women wanted to know about first ladies Jackie and Lady Bird.

Don was with President Kennedy for a year and with President Johnson almost five years. He traveled with the presidents wherever they went and spent a lot of time at Johnson's ranch. He remembers so much about President Johnson, Lady Bird and the two daughters. He related to me once that at ten o'clock in the evening, no matter what they were doing, Mrs. Johnson would stop and go in her bedroom to watch Gun Smoke on her TV. The president always enjoyed showing his guests his prize Bulls.

When I turned seventy years old, my accountant recommended I sell all my cows and retire, leaving the ranches to the boys and their families. I owned cows all my life, how could I sell them? They were part of my life. I brooded over it for a week, and Don told me to stop worrying. Sit down, make a decision and then act on it. I did that and decided that he and my accountant were right. My children were old enough and responsible enough, and their children are getting old enough to help do ranch work. In the end I sold all my cows to the two boys and retired.

We continued to go to the ranch each summer but didn't stay as long as we formerly did. The boys were in charge and they did things their way. They did things differently from what I did and sometimes it bothered me, so my trips became shorter as the years passed.

Chapter "34"

On our second winter together, as a happily married couple, we had planned to spend in the Florida Keys. We stopped overnight in Melbourne Florida and changed our plans. We stayed there until we went back to the ranch in April. Melbourne was the place where the boat salesman wanted to sell me a boat the first time we went to Florida.

I enjoyed it more this year than the previous year and yes, the air is clean and fresh just like Don said it would be. One reason I enjoyed it so much was because some of the people I made friends with last year were there, and I made more new friends this year. It appeared to me that the same people come back to the same campground and stayed in the same space year after year. One lady told me this was her eighteenth winter in this park. She was ninety two years old and in good condition. After we were there a week we found there were a variety of interesting things to do in the park. We rode our bicycles in and out of the park and played several different kinds of games on the ground and grass. Every evening we played card games and on Wednesday night we played bingo. On Sunday there was a church service in the park but we chose to attend the Baptist Church where we made friends last year. We enjoyed Sunday school and the preaching. The music was the good old songs that we all knew. They also had activities for seniors during the week.

The ocean was only a few miles from our campground. We walked the beach once a month and each time I picked up a quart or more of shells to make things out of when I went back to the ranch. We also went square dancing twice a week in the evenings. We went fishing once on a party boat and only caught a few small fish. There were too many people on the boat to have fun and enjoy fishing. We were involved in so many activities that spring seemed to arrive too soon, and it was time to go back to the ranch.

When we returned to the ranch we repeated all the things we normally did when on the ranch plus we went on a trip or two. When the weather turned cool in Wyoming we knew it was time to hook up our Airstream, head for Florida and spend the winter in the sun shine down in the Florida Keys as we planned.

Chapter "35"

We went to Big Pine Key where we rented a camp site for two months. We bought a nineteen foot power boat for fishing, snorkeling and to dive from. Every day we would take it out fishing or just riding. Don was a certified scuba diver and offered to teach me to snorkel. By this time being married to Don was an adventurous, interesting and exciting life so I agreed to learn to snorkel. We went to a dive shop and bought a snorkel, a mask and fins. Being a few miles off shore swimming in the ocean was scary at first but after I learned how, it was fun. About a week later we were snorkeling around a coral head about two miles off shore. Suddenly, Don motioned me away and toward the boat. After we were in the boat, I questioned him as to why we had to board the boat so quickly when we were having so much fun. He asked me? "Didn't you see that shark?" I said no, it's hard for me to see without my glasses. He said I'm glad you told me because it's important that you see well. If you can't see well you miss the beauty of the living ocean and it could also be dangerous. The next day he took me to an optical office in a dive shop. I got tested and we bought glasses to fit inside my mask. What a difference that made. Now I could really see and enjoy snorkeling even more. I looked for sharks but never saw any. I did see schools of large and very beautiful angel fish, parrot fish and all kinds of other sea creatures. It was so exciting that I never wanted to stop looking. Every day we would either go out fishing, snorkeling or just riding in the boat.

When our two months at the campground were up we looked for a house on the island. After a few days we found one that needed some repairs. It was on a canal and only five hundred feet from the Bay and about three miles from the ocean. It was an old house on ground level. The front and back could be opened in case of a hurricane. If a hurricane hit the island you just opened the front and back and let the wind and water go through the house. Houses built since that time are required to be six feet above mean high tide. Most are built eight feet off the ground so you can park a car or truck under the house. We bought the house at a fair price and began to work on it. It had a flat roof that needed repair so that was the first thing we did. We patched and repaired it and then applied two coats of good white roof tar on it. We had our boat so we went fishing and snorkeling when we were tired of working on the house. When Don went deep sea diving I would snorkel over him. The water was so clear I could see one hundred feet down with my mask and snorkel. Sometimes he would shoot a fish for dinner and sometimes he would bring a pretty mussel shell for me to see or keep if we could extract the mussel.

I really liked it here. We made new friends from the Baptist Church and in our local Square Dance Club. We dance twice a week and next year we plan to learn how to round dance. Round dance is done in a circle with a partner and square dance is done in a square with eight people. It is excellent exercise for the body and brain.

It will be summer soon and time to hook up the Airstream and go to the ranch for a few weeks. In the future we plan to go to Wyoming to visit my children, take a sightseeing trip, then go to Minnesota to visit Don's brother and sister, then to Washington, DC to visit Don's children. This year we also went to a square dance festival. We are busy all the time doing fun things and staying young. It seems like there is not enough time to do all the things we want to do.

When it started to get cold we hooked up our Airstream and headed back to Florida and our cozy home on an island. Big Pine Key is about three miles long by four miles wide. When we lived there, there were about one hundred residents.

Chapter "36"

Our home on Big Pine Key was just as we left it. There were things that needed repair but first we had to go for a swim in the canal. The next day we put our power boat in the water and tied it up at our dock. After lunch we took our boat out into the ocean for a ride and a half hour of snorkeling. We bought supplies and started working on our house once again. We worked for about two weeks on the house and had it looking good as new. Then it was time to play some more. Nearly every day we went fishing or snorkeling. Sometimes we fixed a lunch, took the boat out into the ocean, ate our lunch and then, lay down in the boat and tried to take a nap. Being too excited to nap, we would ride for a short time and then went home to take a well-deserved nap.

The house looked good but now it's time to tackle the yard work. We had some sod and grass but had to lay down some new sod. We had to water it for a few days using some very expensive water. Our water came from a well in Homestead Florida, one hundred miles away. Then we bought and planted some tropical shrubs that flower most of the year. Digging a hole for the shrubs was almost impossible because the ground was solid rock. To dig a hole you had to work with a pick axe or some such tool. In just a few months our house and yard were beautiful.

Don wanted to plant a garden, but there was no way to plant anything in such rocky soil. He decided to buy enough concrete blocks to make a ten foot square bed. After a few hard windy days he drove his truck to the ocean shore and picked up enough sea weed that had blown in to fill his new garden. He had it piled about one foot above the blocks. When we arrived the next fall he planted his vegetable seeds in the dead sea weed. I gently informed him that he planted too many seeds and too close together. Much to my surprise, in a few weeks we were eating the best vegetables we had ever eaten. That little garden produced far more than we could eat. He repeated the same thing for the next three years and always had a very successful garden.

We attended a Baptist Church and enjoyed our church friends. Don became involved as a greeter and usher, and I volunteered in the Nursey. I held and rocked the little babies. What a joy. They called me the rocking grandma. In a few weeks all the young children knew me and wanted me to rock them. Unfortunately, my lap wasn't big enough to hold more than one unless they were very small.

We square danced twice a week and started round dance lessons. Round dancing is a style of dance that was featured on the Lawrence Welk show. The lessons took most of the afternoon. Our teacher let us record what he taught so when we got home we could practice what we learned until we perfected it. We became good round dancers in a very short time. We continued taking lessons until we were in a high level of dancing. Both dancers and non-dancers enjoyed watching us dance. A few years later an advertising company made a film of us round dancing. It was shown on television as an advertisement for a pizza place and another restaurant. We also appeared in the local newspaper.

Chapter "37"

We spent the summer visiting in Wyoming, Minnesota and Washington, DC. Then we went to an Airstream Rally and did some sightseeing. When cold weather was on the margin we headed back to Florida.

Our to-do list remained the same. Swim in the canal, work on the house, put the boat in the water, go fishing, snorkeling, scuba diving and plant a garden. It's called living life to the fullest.

We faced one problem. We had not painted the bottom of our boat. When left in salt water, if you don't use special bottom paint, barnacles and mermaid hair will grow on the bottom. Barnacles and mermaid hair will make the boat feel as if it is dragging something. We made plans to have a boat lift installed next year. After that painting the bottom will no longer be necessary. We contracted to have it done because the ground was hard as a rock. The next year when the contractor arrived he had a big tractor with a large drill or auger. He drilled two big holes about twenty-five feet apart and about six feet deep. Then he put iron rods in the holes and then filled the holes with concrete. After the concrete dried he put a three foot square frame on the top and filled those with concrete. While the concrete was still wet, he put four large two foot long bolts with a curve in the bottom in each frame. When the concrete was dry he put the boat lifts or davits over the bolts. Don did the electrical wiring. Then he took the tires off the boat trailer and set the trailer under the lift. How wonderful it was to come back from fishing or diving and just push a button to lift the boat out of the water and place it on the trailer where it was secure, dry and never needed bottom paint.

Chapter "38"

One evening when we were square dancing a friend, whom Don knew for years, asked us if we would like to go out for a sailboat ride with him and his wife. He knew Don had a small sailboat before he met me. We said we would love to go for a ride on his sailboat. That was another new experience for me. We took water and a little lunch along for all of us. We boarded his sailboat about ten o'clock and were out in the ocean by eleven o'clock. Immediately I loved it. It was so quiet and smooth not like our power boat. I sat in the cockpit and then moved up on the deck. Absolutely exhilarating! Next Don said, go below and see if you like it there. No matter where I sat in the boat, I did not have a problem with seasickness. We ate our lunch and were home by three o'clock. We loved our power boat but sailing was so different, and I loved it. Don proceeded to tell me that the sailboat was only twenty feet long and could be towed from place to place on a trailer, but it was too small to spend the night on and it was limited to traveling only a short distance. Then he asked me?

How would you like a big sailboat that you could live on and sail as far as you want? I thought about that for one whole second and answered, "Are you crazy"? Leave our nice home here, with a good vegetable garden, power boat and so many friends.

I hoped he would never bring that subject up again, but a month later one of his friends told us he was going to a boat show in Miami and invited us to go along with him. We said sure, it will be something new to see and do.

I never saw so many boats in my life and all very shiny and beautiful. I happened to see the price tag on some of them, I told Don if we bought one of those boats, I would have to sell my ranch to pay for it. He assured me that we would never own something like those, so there was no need to worry. The boats ranged from thirty feet long to one hundred feet long, both power and sail. I wanted to board one but the salesman told us we needed deck shoes or we could take off our street shoes. We took off our street shoes and went inside three or four of them. They were so inviting, clean and shiny, but I wanted to get out of there before I feel in love with one. But, I could not help but wonder. What would it be like to sail a big boat like one of these out in the ocean and go to other countries and explore remote islands.

Three months later as we were securing our boat and getting ready to go back north for the summer, Don brought up the subject of a sailboat. I must admit I thought about it a few times myself. We talked about it and decided that when we returned in the fall we will talk about it again. In the meantime Don managed to find a sailboat catalog. Sailboats of every kind and size were listed for sale up and down the east, west and south coast of the United States. I wondered why there were so many sailboats for sale. Later I discovered that instead of the boat owner repairing their boats, they sold them for anything they could get.

Traveling and visiting the ranch and family in Minnesota made sailboats a world apart so the subject didn't come up again.

This summer on the ranch we did the same as past years. Ranch work, Airstream Rally, a trip and this year we ate lunch a few times at the Senior Center. After the meal I played cards with some of my friends that I have known for years. Don went to the Library to read which is his favorite past time. In Minnesota we visited family, some old friends and always played cards.

When cold weather came we again hooked up our Airstream and headed for Florida.

Chapter "39"

It felt great getting back to our cozy home and our power boat. We put the boat in the water and went out in the ocean for a swim and snorkeling. What a life we are living. We worked hard all our lives, and it was worth it.

The next day Don planted his garden that he had filled with sea weed the previous spring. We went fishing and caught enough to have for dinner. There is nothing better than fresh fish right out of the ocean. We only brought about five pounds of red meat from the ranch since coming to Florida. I still enjoy my red meat, but Don would rather have fish or turkey breast and his vegetables.

At square dancing our friend with the sailboat asked us, if we ever thought about trading our power boat for a sailboat. We told him no, because we were satisfied with our power boat. On our way home Don asked me? How would you like to live on a sailboat and sail out and away for months or years? I answered, that would really be different but I don't know if I could survive that long. He reminded me that he was a boat captain, knew how to read a chart, plot a course and navigate. He assured me he was also a licensed radio operator and knew how to get the weather forecast by radio when sailing out in the ocean. The small sailboat he had was suitable only for day sailing, but if we had one as big or bigger than the Airstream, we could sail for a month or more and return home at will.

I agreed to look into the purchase of a sailboat. For the next two years we looked up and down both coasts of Florida. The boats we looked at were old, too highly priced and in need of much repair. The first one we looked at was in Fort Lauderdale. It was a thirty seven foot Endeavor Sloop. It would be big enough for us to live on and small enough for the two of us to safely sail. It was ten years old and never used. The couple who bought it had good intentions but their parents became ill and they had to take care of them until they died. Nine years after they bought it, they stopped making payments and the bank repossessed it. While looking at boats and talking too many of salesmen we found that a boat that floats in the water for ten years either had blisters or will have them very soon. In time, sea water leaks through the gel coat and causes blisters.

After looking at over a hundred boats in a span

of more than two years we noticed that the boat we had first looked at in Fort Lauderdale was still for sale and the bank had reduced the price. Originally, the boat cost over two hundred thousand dollars. Now the asking price was twenty thousand. We looked at it again. This time very carefully and found the sails, engine and all lines were new, and still in excellent condition. The salesman took us out in the ocean for a sail and we fell in love with it, even though we knew it would require much work before we could take it on a long trip.

We had it surveyed for insurance purposes which took one day. According to the report, everything was in good condition with one exception; it had a bad case of blisters. That night we discussed the pros and cons of buying this boat. We bought it the next day.

We returned to Big Pine Key and that night I called my children and told them that we had just purchased a big sailboat. Each of them asked me whether I was crazy and was the Florida sun baking my brain.

Chapter"40"

A friend drove us back to Fort Lauderdale to get our new sailboat. The marina was on a channel about one mile from the ocean. We motored to the ocean, put up the sails and headed for home, a three day trip. We anchored out near shore and stayed overnight twice. We tried to use the stove to make a meal on the first night but the stove did not work. Maybe I was crazy to agree with the decision to buy the boat. We started the generator and used the microwave. It worked, but from the beginning we knew, because of the low price, we were headed for some serious work.

We had never experienced anything like this in our lives, but with twenty thousand precious dollars invested, we would need to learn to love it. Don assured me that the more we sail that the better we would like it. We anchored it in the bay near our home and finally reached home by Dinghy. We pulled the dinghy up on our lawn and sat down. We looked at each other and I said, "What did we get ourselves into now?"

The next day we took our power boat out to the

sailboat, sat in it, and looked at it and began making plans to dry dock it to remove the blisters. Before we went home we went fishing and had a little swim but our hearts were not in it. We now owned a sailboat that needed our undivided attention.

The following day we went to Key West and made arrangements to have our sailboat dry docked. The boat yard manager instructed us as to what we had to do to remove the blisters.

First it would have to sit on supports in the boatyard for five or six months to dry out. When it was dry, all the blisters would be visible because they will still be wet. All the time the boat yard manager was talking, Don was writing. When he had finished talking, Don had half of a five by seven pad filled. I know we were facing many hours of hard work but we thought it would be fun, exciting and quite a challenge, because we had never done anything like this in our lives. Did I say challenge? Fun? I was a rancher, not a sailboat repair girl but, it was our boat. Welcome to the boating world, ranch girl!

The day after we talked to the boatyard manager, we sailed our sailboat to Key West and had it put in storage to dry out. The marina has a boat slip that you drive your boat into. That is where it is taken out and put back in the water when the repairs have been made.

The machine they used to take it out of the water was a big square frame tractor with the engine on the side and belts on the bottom. The boat yard manager placed the belts under our boat in such a way so they would not touch the depth sounder or engine exhaust. He then lifted it up out of the water and drove it to the storage area. What a sight that was to watch. That big tractor was carrying our sailboat down the road a quarter of a mile to the storage area! When he got our boat to the storage area, he put supports under our boat so it would be stable enough for us to move around on it safely as we worked and to withstand a strong wind.

Five months later the bottom was dry so we began working on our boat. There was no electricity in the storage area so we bought about five hundred feet of electric cable to go from our boat to an electrical outlet in the marina. Don got out his note pad and studied all the instructions that the boat yard manager gave him. With a large hand held grinder Don started grinding out the blisters. Some were so deep and wide he had to be careful not to go through the hull of the boat. The next step was to fill all of the holes with epoxy putty. There must have been twenty or more. The putty dries very quickly and because it is very expensive Don had to be prepared and work fast. After the putty was set and leveled he applied an epoxy gel coat. It also dries fast and is very expensive. Then he put on a marine paint premier and finally he applied the finish coat of paint. When everything was dry, he cleaned the complete bottom of the boat by sanding it with fine sandpaper, on a little hand held sander until it is smooth. Then it was ready to paint the part of the boat that is under the water with a top grade under water marine paint. While he was busy with the blister problem and the painting, I worked on the teak wood, both on the inside and outside, and all the stainless steel. We worked every day for eight hours a day. The whole process took us a little less than one year including the time in storage. The dry dock fee was less than we thought because our boat was out in the storage area and not in the boatyard. Our sailboat looked brand new. All we had to do was put the name of the boat on the stern along with the port city. We named our boat "QUEEN BEE." The port city was "KEY WEST,

FLORIDA." Large boats are not registered with the state but are documented by United States government. Once documented, wherever you take your boat, they are not interested in you, the owner, only the boat, so they go by the boat name.

The time finally arrived to put our beautiful sailboat back in the water to keep the bottom paint from deteriorating. The boatyard manager brought his big tractor to our boat, lifted it up and carried it the quarter mile to the boat slip and put it back into the water.

Chapter "41"

We sailed to a local marina and tied up to the dock. People came from everywhere to see our boat and talk about it. It looked like new and they thought we were wealthy to have such a boat. We discovered that only a few people actually traveled anywhere in them. They lived on their boats but always seemed to have sailing stories, probably heard them from real sailors. A few that lived on their boat had a job in town. There back grounds were vastly different from mine. Most were retired from the Navy but a few had retired from other branches of the military. One was a retired doctor, one was a retired preacher. One boat owner was a retired pilot. Most of them were married and the few that were not were looking for wives who enjoyed sailing. They all had stories to tell. I think I'll like it here. Living with Don was so different than I was accustomed to and so exciting. There was never a dull moment. His brain never stopped.

We still had our beautiful home on Big Pine Key. As much as we liked our home, it was time to put it on the market. I thought the asking price the realtor suggested was too inflated. Don said we could reduce it if there was a prospective buyer. We continued living in our house, going fishing, snorkeling, diving and every time we went to the sailboat we would take something with us. Moving in a little at a time and visiting with our new friends.

A few months later we sold our home for our asking price and I must admit, at a hefty profit. The buyers also wanted everything in our house. Not only did we get our asking price we sold them everything in our house at a fair price. One week later we went to closing and they moved in as we were moving out our remaining personal things.

After we moved our personal effects into the boat all we had left was our pickup truck and our Airstream trailer. We kept our truck in the marina parking lot for transportation and we put our Airstream in storage. For a home address we rented a mail box in Key West. For a year we had no telephone but later we bought a cell phone that had intermittent service.

Every day was a new day with new experiences. Boat people don't wear spiffy uptown clothes so we resorted to wearing our old clothes. Some boat people look like real bums, but are actually just very relaxed, educated and care free people.

Chapter "42"

Life in the marina was good. We would visit other boat people and maybe go to town for lunch. Don enjoyed eating in the boat so he could maintain his diet of fruit and vegetables, with very little red meat. Some boat people, most of them active sailors, lived in their boats out in the bay rather than in the marina. Every day they would come in for happy hour or go to town to shop or do their laundry. They had no additional expenses and were away from all the noise and people. Don and I talked about it and agreed to try living on the boat out in the bay. When our rent was up in the marina we went out to the bay and enjoyed it out there much more than at the dock although we didn't have electricity or fresh water. We did have a wind charger, a generator and four large batteries for electric. Whenever we went to the marina dinghy dock we would take back five gallons of fresh water. For a small fee the marina allowed us use the dinghy dock, park our truck in the parking lot, get water for our boat and use the marina showers. We had a shower on the boat, but the shower in the marina was bigger, the water was heated, and it was something different to do. We also went to happy hour every day where everyone enjoyed an alcoholic drink, a soft drink or water along with a snack. There was talk about every subject. We learned and shared.

Some of the active sailors were very knowledgeable about sailing. We were planning a shakedown trip and wanted all the knowledge we could gather. Don knew all about sailing but his boat was smaller and he only had day sailing experience. We were planning to be gone for a week on this, our first trip.

We discovered that when you sail, because of the weather conditions you can't plan on sailing for just two days or a week. There were times we waited a week or more for good wind and weather.

Chapter "43"

Our first trip or shakedown trip would be to the Dry Tortugas. (Fort Jefferson). Don bought a chart and plotted a course. We also went to the library to learn more about the Dry Tortugas.

The day we set sail the weather and the wind speed were perfect and the wind was coming from the right direction. About halfway to our destination, we stopped at an uninhabited island. We took our dinghy in and beach combed for a while. After finding an old bottle and some interesting shells we returned to the boat. We were in our boat for about ten minutes when we saw a very large Devil Ray swim by within two feet of our boat. It was so beautiful with its big wings going up and down so slowly and gracefully. Is this what sailing is all about? It was peaceful and quiet. We decided to stay and sleep near the island overnight and set sail again tomorrow.

On our second day to the Dry Tortugas we encountered a storm making waves about fifteen feet high. It came up so quickly we didn't have time to drop the sails. As Don was feverishly trying to get them down I was at the wheel. Sailing was not fun now. I wanted to go home. I looked back and saw a large cargo ship not far from us. Don was still trying to lower the sails when I yelled to him that there was a ship about to run over us!! In seconds he had the sails down and the motor was running. He grabbed the radio and called the big ship on marine channel sixteen. They assured us we were on their radar and that we are safe. Then they gave us some good news. "You will be out of the storm in about fifteen minutes." They were right but that fifteen minutes seemed like two hours. It was our first storm and I hoped it was our last. At that time I felt like selling the boat and buying another house. How did I get myself in this situation?

After the storm abated Don engaged the auto pilot and hoisted the sails. Then he gave me a big hug, held me and talked to me. He told me to trust in God, believe in yourself and listen to your heart. Without trust we imprison our joy. I knew what he was saying made a lot of sense and I started thinking. I knew if I let fear over take me, my pleasure trip would be doomed. Fear to a great extent is born from stories you hear, so I chose to tell myself a different story. I decided I was safe. I was strong. I could not be defeated. I will not let the Devil steal my pleasure. I am a saved Christian. I know God will not give me more than I can handle. Thinking such as that is a form of mind control, positive thinking. I will not allow myself to be afraid. Fear begets fear. It wasn't long until all my fears subsided. I don't know what I imagined sailing would be like but I do know from now on I will enjoy it.

After the storm Don checked the entire boat and discovered only one problem, a leaky porthole which he could easily fix. He admitted to learning a very good lesson. Watch the sky and every cloud. Had he done that, he would have dropped the main sail and brought in the jib to a small triangle. He related that this was the purpose of the trip, to remind him of the things he once knew but had forgotten.

We anchored in the Bay of Fort Jefferson on Dry Tortugas. The only way to get there is by boat or sea plane. It is located about seventy miles from Key West. We went ashore and toured the old fort. Before we left Key West we went to the library to get information about the fort.

Dry Tortugas is composed of a cluster of islands discovered in 1513. It is famous for its coral reef, Bird Island, marine life and its many legends of pirates and sunken gold. It is named for a large population of turtles that live in the area.

The United States Government started building Fort Jefferson in 1846 to protect the south eastern coast of the United States. The brick and all supplies were brought in by boat from all over Florida and later from the entire southeastern United States and as far north as Maine. Sixteen million bricks were used in the building of the fort but more were needed. Because of the weight of the bricks, mortar and lumber, the island and the fort began to sink. The work was ceased and the fort was never finished or used as a fort.

This Fort was later used as a prison. It was the place where Doctor Mudd was imprisoned in 1865 for conspiring to assassinate President Abraham Lincoln. When an epidemic of yellow fever gripped the fort two years later, the Doctor helped to save the lives of the soldiers who guarded him. This eventually earned him his pardon from President Andrew Johnson.

After we finished sightseeing, Don checked the weather and was happy to report that the first day of our return trip would be good sailing but on the second day the wind would be on the bow. We couldn't sail under those conditions so our choices were to stay put or go under motor. Don, being a sailor, preferred to sail one day and then anchor in the bay of another uninhabited island, explore the island, beachcomb and read a book. That's what we decided to do. Unfortunately, the weather was bad for almost a week. We fished, played cards, and read some from the books we brought with us. I caught a nice hammerhead shark about two feet long. We skinned it, cut it up and ate it with great delight, noting there were no bones in it. Finally, the weather turned favorable for sailing and we set sail for home.

Reflecting on this trip I must say we learned much about sailing, and except for the storm, we had a wonderful experience on our first sailing trip to the Dry Tortugas. I believe we are ready for an extended trip.

Chapter "44"

Back in Key West we anchored in the Bay as we did before and went ashore in our dinghy. Our sailing friends were curious about our trip. After we related all our experiences, those who had never been there wanted to get several other boats together and make the trip. Most sailors like to travel with their drinking buddies. We do not drink so we prefer to sail alone. If we need help we have radios. One radio will go about fifty miles, the other one will reach around the world.

Don fixed the leaky porthole and started talking about a much longer trip. It was January now, the hurricane season was over and it would be a good time to sail farther south where it would be warmer. Don acquired more charts and we discussed sailing to the Bahamas. The Bahamas are a coral based archipelago in the Atlantic Ocean. It has seven hundred plus islands, cays and islets. They range from uninhabited to islands packed with resorts. It is officially known as the Commonwealth of the Bahamas. Columbus made his first landfall in the new world in the Bahamas in 1492.

Another boat wanted to sail with us and being this was our first long trip we welcomed them to join us. Don plotted a course then watched the weather. He checked with the weather station by VHF and HF radio twice a day if bad weather was coming in or once a day if the weather was good. Near the end of January the weather looked favorable so we weighed anchor at eleven o'clock in the morning and set sail. We sailed all day and got in the golf stream, picked up speed, sailed all night and arrived at South Riding Rock at eight o'clock the next morning. Sailing at night was a gratifying experience. The moon was so bright you could read a newspaper. Don took the first watch and I tried to sleep but couldn't. I was just too excited. At midnight I took over the watch, and Don slept for about two hours. South Riding Rock is a very small island about one hundred feet wide and five hundred feet long, six feet high and sits on a reef. One side of the island is over one thousand feet deep. After you very carefully cross over and through the cut in the reef, it was about sixty feet deep.

We anchored on the sixty foot side and ate breakfast. Don went diving for lobster along the reef. He found two and we ate them for lunch. Then he dived straight down under our boat and found a conch bed with very old conch. The lip of the conch was an inch or more thick. He brought up a couple and checked the mussel to see if it was good. It was old but tasted the same as a small one so he kept diving until we had enough conch meat for a month. He dived all morning bringing up two or three each time. In the afternoon we cleaned them and put most of them in our freezer. We put the remainder in our refrigerator to eat within the next several days. We slept there that night and set sail the next morning. That night we slept on what the chart called the banks. It was out in the ocean away from everything and only about thirty five feet deep. At night if you are sailing or anchored and asleep, you must have a light on top of the mast so other boats can see you are a sailboat. We awoke at six o'clock, ate breakfast and set sail. The water was so clear you could easily see sea fans, ocean sponges, small fish and other sea life. Sailing across that kind of water is like watching a movie, set in the ocean. It is so beautiful and interesting. Eventually, we arrived at Chub Cay, the first Island we came to in the Bahamas. We cleared customs and immigrations and stayed at the dock overnight. We heard on the weather radio there was a bad storm coming so we sailed to a bigger and higher island called Whale Cay. It was shaped like a horse shoe and protected from the wind on three sides. We were safe until another boat arrived. It was a new fifty two foot sailboat. When they anchored I knew from the beginning they didn't know what they were doing. We could be in trouble. After they anchored the husband and wife came over to our boat for a visit. They informed us that they had just bought their boat and this was their first trip. I attempted to tell them they were improperly anchored and if a storm came it could send them adrift. He didn't listen. He was a "know it all!" A storm did come and when it reached its peak it sent his boat adrift. As he passed us he pulled our two anchors out and set us adrift. We landed on a sandy beach, and he landed on the rocks. When the storm abated, we waited for high tide, put our anchor out in the deep water and pulled ourselves out. Then, set sail for our next adventure. Our only damage was to our bottom paint. When we left they were still on the rocks calling for the Coast Guard on the radio requesting a tow boat to get them off the rocks. A few weeks later we heard on the radio that they had lost their boat by running up on a reef.

From there we sailed to New Providence Island. Before we entered the Port we must call Harbor Control and ask permission to enter. When a large vessel is going out or preparing to go out, Harbor Control orders the boat captain to stand off until called. No ships were coming out so we received permission to enter and anchored in the Bay. The police station was located on the water front and had a dinghy dock for sailors who wanted to visit the city.

We took our dinghy in, secured it to the dinghy dock and spent the day walking, riding the city bus and eating in a local restaurant. The food was different but very good. Everyone was friendly and we enjoyed our conversations with them. The time came to return to the boat. It was a full day and I was dead tired!

The next day we ate breakfast in the cockpit. We sat there listening to the chatter on the VHF radio and the local radio. It was a busy port with big ships constantly coming and going. We stayed busy for the next five days sightseeing and resting. On our way back to our boat on our last day in town a couple waved us down to talk. When I noticed that their dinghy was a flat bottom aluminum boat I knew they were not sailors. In talking to them we found out he was a retired Navy Officer but knew nothing about sailing. He said his wife took a course but she is not doing very well. He wanted to know where we were going and asked permission to follow us. We told them we were planning to sail to Norman Cay then go on to The Great Exuma Islands. Our plan was to set sail the next morning about nine o'clock. He promised they would be ready. At nine o'clock we pulled anchor and motored out of the bay. As we passed them they were ready and fell in behind us. I noticed they had a thirty five foot day sailor with a small engine. Once we were out of the bay we hosted sail and I noticed they were falling behind. They finally put up their sails but were falling farther behind. We called them on the VHF radio and advised them to motor sail or they would not arrive at Norman Cay until after dark which would be unsafe. There was a reef at the island where day light was needed in order to pass through the cut. One hour later I looked back and could barely see them. The bottom of their boat must have been really dirty. They arrived after dark and anchored outside the island. During the night a hard wind came up and they rocked and rolled all night. The next day when I called them on the radio, they said they were returning to the States. Going to sea in a day sailor or a racer is not a good idea.

An ocean going craft and sailing knowledge is absolutely required in order to have fun and be safe on the ocean. In our seven years of sailing, we saw a lot of sailors who should have stayed home because they were not equipped with the knowledge needed to enjoy ocean sailing.

On the way to the Great Exuma we stopped at another uninhibited island called Bell Island. We stayed there for three days and did a little exploring, fishing and snorkeling. It was exciting to be there where no one had been since the days of slavery. We saw a few old stone homes that had half fallen down, a stone walk-way, and fences made from stone. We watched some birds and long colorful lizards. It was all very exciting. We wanted to stay longer but the wind was coming from the right direction and we needed to locate some fresh vegetables so we set sail and went to the Great Exuma Islands.

When we arrived, there were other sailors in the Bay from all over the states and other countries. There was no dock to tie up to but there was a large dinghy dock. We anchored in the bay, took our dinghy into the dock and walked around the island. It was a large island with several towns on it. The largest was Georgetown. It had a grocery store, a hardware store, a drinking water plant, post office, police station and two churches. There were water wells on the island, but no one drank that water. It had too much salt in it and was used for washing clothes, dishes, and flushing the toilet.

We stayed there two weeks. One Sunday we went to the Baptist church in Georgetown. The service started at nine o'clock in the morning. They prayed, sang and preached until noon. The only instrument they had was an organ. When the organist played a song with a beat, everybody did a little dance step in place. Obviously they enjoyed their church service to the fullest extent.

Lunch followed the church service and in the same building. They invited us to have lunch with them and we accepted. They served chicken with peas and rice which was one of their favorite meals. It was excellent. In the afternoon the service commenced again. We attended that service for half an hour then went back to our boat.

We enjoyed the service but it was certainly different from any other church service we had attended. The one thing I remember was, they really like to sing and were very good at it. The one song they sang that I will never forget was: "Our God Reigns." They had an organ and an organist who was very talented but that song they sang without the organ. Don said they don't sing by note, they sing by letter. They just open their mouth and let-her out. We loved it.

After we left the church we had to laugh at ourselves. When the service started the Pastor said, I see we have a couple foreigners with us. Would you please stand and tell us your name and where you are from. We looked around to see who the foreigners were. Then it hit us! We are the foreigners.

When we were not sailing at night, Don and I would play cards or dominos. Sometimes I thought he allowed me to win at cards but when it came to dominos, I usually beat him. Then he would accuse me of cheating. If we had a chance to trade books with other sailors, we might read instead of playing cards. I also did a lot of fancy needle work while on the boat.

The island next to us was about two miles away and was mostly sand. It was named Stocking Island and every day the sailors would dinghy over there to play all kinds of games. We enjoyed it here but since this was our first trip we wanted to sail more and see more. When the wind came from the right direction we set sail. We stopped at another uninhabited island on our way called Lee Stocking Cay. It was a small island with nothing to see. We fished, swam, and cleaned the boat. We spent only three days there then set sail again. When we caught a fish we filleted it, washed it in the ocean water and put it in the frying pan. I never tasted better fish. Three or four weeks later we stopped in Nassau. We walked around and did the usual tourist thing. One young American couple stopped us and warned us that two guys had just stolen their gold neck chains and for us to be careful. We told them that the way we looked everybody would be afraid of us. We and other boat people look and feel like homeless bums but in fact, most are well educated and lived on boats worth over one hundred thousand dollars. We definitely did not look very wealthy. Most active sailors had a dark tan and haven't had a hair cut in months. They looked more like refugees. Can you picture Don, a gentleman who worked in the White House, lived in a coat and tie and now looked homeless? The bottom line was, we loved our life on the boat.

A week later we left Nassau, sailed to Chub Cay, cleared customs and then anchored in the Bay waiting for good weather so we could make our crossing to the states. We sat there for eight days just waiting for good weather. While waiting, we went with our dinghy looking for lobster and conch. We found some conch but no lobster. The conch we eat are the queen conch but today Don found a horse conch. They have a colorful shell but are completely different from a queen and do not taste good. He also found a nice little Seahorse in the seaweed. He brought it up to show me then put it back.

From Chub Cay to home there was no place to

get out of a storm and no place to wait if the wind changed directions. Sailors are prepared for such developments. They always have a stack of books available to read. Whenever we made land fall, we traded books with other sailors.

A few months ago we lost our wind for three hours while sailing. We jumped in the ocean for a swim and took a bath. Got back in the boat, rinsed off with fresh water and took a nap. At that place the ocean was over ten thousand feet deep so we didn't worry about stepping on anything.

Fair wind coming from the right direction was predicted. We weighed anchor at eight o'clock in the morning and set sail. We took the long way home and five days later we reached Key West. We cleared customs and anchored in the bay as we had done on previous trips.

We took our dinghy in and tied up at the dinghy dock. Before we were completely tied up several boating friends came to greet us. It was so good to see them again. We had happy hour early that day because in a very short time a crowd had gathered. They were curious about our trip, where we went and what we did. There was so much chatter and so many questions that it was difficult to relate our stories. Now that I know what sailing the seas was all about, I am anxiously looking forward to our next trip.

Some of the active sailors were still overseas and several found employment in town. One started school under the GI Bill. There were a few new boaters and then there were those who sold their boat and went north.

It was the end of May and the weather was hot. Those who lived on their boat in the bay wore the least amount of clothes possible. When visiting friends on other boats it was advisable to announce your approach by calling out to them.

Having been out to sea for five months, putting on respectable clothes to go to town or church felt strange. Driving down US 1 was also strange to Don because he was having difficulty getting the truck to run over fifteen miles per hour. When we sailed our speed was between three and six miles per hour. To us, fifteen miles per hour was really flying. When we were in the Gulf Stream we did six and seven but as soon as we left it, we would be down to about five. We were never in a hurry, it's impossible on a sailboat.

When we sailed Don put the auto pilot on then sat and read a book. While he read I would fish. Some days I caught so many I had to throw them back into the ocean. If I caught a big one Don would help me bring it aboard. One time I caught a big one and when I reeled it in close to the boat, Don tried to gaff it to pull it aboard. The gaff didn't hook it well enough and the fish took off. It took me twenty minutes to get it back to the boat. This time Don was able to gaff it and pull it aboard.

Chapter "45"

There wasn't much for us to do in Key West so we hooked up our Airstream to our Truck and headed to my ranch in Wyoming and Don's family in Minnesota.

Life at the ranch changed. My boys have their own ideas which in some cases are different from mine.

We went to an Airstream Rally and few sightseeing trips. We went square dancing in Casper every Saturday night and once in Cheyanne. We ate lunch at the Senior Center a few times and I played cards with my friends after lunch while Don went to the Library.

Don and I rode the horses out on the ranch and again Don was all eye's looking for old things that were lost or thrown away by early travelers. He always found a few small stones that he wanted to keep. He thought that someday he might have a ring made with a beautiful little stone that he found on the ranch. Every summer he would find an arrow head or what looked like an arrow head.

In Minnesota, Don always enjoyed his brother, sister and their families. They always had stories about their child hood days. I think some stories the boys told were a little stretched because their sister just looked away.

We read an assortment of sailing magazines and Don tried to teach me navigation. In the end I think I could plot a course and navigate if necessary. Since he was a licensed radio operator, he taught me how to use the HF radio and all about the different frequencies. Before our first trip he taught me how to use the VHF radio. The VHF radio is good for about fifty miles and can be used to call the coast guard. The HF radio will go around the world but you are required to use the frequencies you are licensed to use.

When it started to cool down Don was ready to go to Florida and to our sailboat. He had plans to change some things and he couldn't wait to get back and get started on his projects. He also acquired more nautical charts and began plotting a course for our next trip. He wanted to leave the states as soon as hurricane season ends. I was in no hurry. I had enjoyed my friends in Wyoming, in Minnesota, as well as at the marina in Florida, square dancing and in our church. I was doing so many different things and having so much fun that I couldn't get it all in. Don is very good for me, and also very understanding. He always refers to us as a team.

Chapter "46"

As soon as we arrived in Key West we put our Airstream in storage and went to the boat. It was the same as when we left it, at its home base. Don wanted to take it out in the ocean for a day of sailing but I talked him out of it. There is too much involved to take it out for only one day. After the long trip from Wyoming and Minnesota, I just want to rest for a few days, swim, and visit with my friends.

After we were here a few weeks Don made arrangements with the boat yard to have our boat hauled out so he could clean and repaint the bottom. He ordered a new depth sounder that he wanted to install when the boat was in the boatyard. He began taking measurements to build a navigation station which would be placed in the cockpit at the helm. He planned to build it the next summer at the ranch where he would have the proper tools. When he is finish our boat would be better than new. We have everything in our boat that we had in our house on the ranch except a dish washer but Don always helped me wash dishes so I didn't mind. Our generator and wind charger gave us all the electricity we needed to keep our batteries fully charged in order to run the refrigerator/freezer and all of our electronics. We had an electric water heater plus the water was automatically heated when the engine ran. When we were out to sea we would hang a plastic water bag full of sea water on the boom. When it's warm or hot we opened the little hose/nozzle on the end to take a shower, after which we used a garden sprayer with fresh water to rinse off the salt. When we are in port we put a curtain around the cockpit for privacy. We had a fifty gallon fresh water tank and when it rained we filled our tank. We were never without fresh water. We took twenty gallons of drinking water in separate containers aboard when we left the States. When the water supply was depleted we purchased drinking water from a drinking water plant, when we stopped at the next inhabited island.

The time had come to have our boat hauled out with that big square framed tractor. This time the yard manager put us in the boat yard. There we have water and electricity and could live on our boat while working on it. It was on supports so we used a ten foot ladder to get in and out of our boat. We did our own work on the boat which saves us some money. The charge for being in the boat yard began the first day so we began our work that very day. Don started cleaning the bottom, preparatory to painting it. He also cleaned, waxed and polished the sides all around. My job was to clean and treat all the teak and clean and polish the bright work. Don and I worked long hard hours for seven days and finished our jobs about the same time, but there is one more thing to do: go up the fifty foot mast to check the light, antennas, and pulleys. Don attached a Boatswain's chair to a line and I had to winch him up to the mast head. He took a line with him and if he needed a tool or something, he would lower the line and I attached the item to it and he would pull it up. When he was finished he said, "Winch me down very slowly." I said, do you promise to wash the dishes for a week? He answered, just lower me down or I'll come down there and throw you in the ocean. I said, how are you going to come down and throw me in the ocean, when you are fifty feet in the air? Then he said, okay, I love you and I'll do anything you want, just winch me down, and very slowly. With us life was never boring.

Now was time to have our boat put back in the water. How beautiful, clean and shiny it was.

We motored back to the bay and anchored near our friends. Don started his annual boat maintenance such as changing the oil and filters in the diesel engine and generator. It was quite challenging to change the oil. Don claimed one had to be half monkey and half snake because it was so difficult to maneuver the body under the cockpit to get to the engine and generator. While he was working I cleaned the inside of the boat, after which I read a good book. We had half a tank of diesel but Don wanted it full before we left. Our generator and engine both ran on diesel. We bought a five gallon diesel can and each time we went to town we brought back a can full of diesel. Every time we went to the dinghy dock we brought bring back four, one gallon milk jugs of water. Two gallons were for drinking and cooking and two were for the fresh water tank. When we were low on fresh water, we washed dishes with salt water and rinsed with fresh water. Life was so different for me but also very exciting with Don. Every day was a new day with different experiences. I, the Wyoming rancher enjoyed every minute of it and looking for more.

Chapter "47"

The hurricane season was ended and we were ready to go. Don had plotted the course and the boat was ready. At happy hour we bid our friends farewell, telling them we were leaving as soon as the weather was good enough for a crossing. A new couple we had never met before wanted to sail with us. They said this would be their first sailing trip. When they said that they had a big dog we were not too sure about sailing with them and their dog. They followed us back to the boat in their dinghy. When we reached their boat, we noticed it was a thirty foot boat and yes, there was a big dog. Seeing that, Don told them that they could follow us but we would not wait for them. With a small boat and a big dog, there is a very good chance they would turn around and head for home within a week. They didn't sail with us. When we returned the next summer we were told that they were gone for two weeks, returned, sold their boat and went north to find a job and a house.

In a few weeks it would be Christmas and our church had big plans for the holiday celebration, so we decided to wait until after Christmas to set sail.

A week after Christmas the weather and wind were favorable so we left our anchorage at eleven o'clock planning to arrive at South Riding Rock at sun up. After we weighted anchor and started motoring out of our anchorage, my shoe came off and went overboard. It was a deck shoe so it floated. Don stopped the boat and began backing it down toward my shoe. I took the boat hook and after fifteen minutes I fished it out. When we entered the Gulf Stream it was running faster than Don had planned but that would be no problem. We would get to South Riding Rock sooner than planned. If we did arrive when it was dark, we would just stand off until there is enough light to cross the reef. Usually Don took the first watch. At midnight he wakened me to take the second watch. At night we sailed with only half of our sails up to be safe. Also the person on watch wore a safety jacket tethered to the boat. Before Don went to sleep we would have a little snack and listen to some church music or a preaching tape we had brought along with us.

We arrived at South Riding Rock as planned. After anchoring in the sixty foot deep water Don went diving for lobster. He only found one but found enough conchs to last us a month.

It was too early for me to go to bed so Don made a line for me to shark fish. I baited the hook and waited. Ten minutes later I caught a shark. It was a big shark about ten feet long. What should I do with it I asked myself? It would be good eating but we don't need it. Don gave me the cable cutter and said he would pull it up as far as he could and I should cut the line. He pulled and I cut the line just an inch from a big row of sharp teeth.

The next day we set sail and stopped at four o'clock, anchored on the flats, had supper and went to bed early. All day the water was only about thirty feet deep and you could clearly see the bottom with all the sea plants and a few small tropical fish. We slept until sunup, ate breakfast and set sail again. Each year sailing over the flats is the same but never boring because there is so much to see. We cleared customs at Chub Cay and anchored in the Bay. After breakfast the next day we set sail for Nassau harbor arriving late in the day. We stayed there for a week sightseeing, eating, walking and visiting with other sailors. There is so much to see in Nassau. We went on a walking tour first then on a bus tour. We saw several beautiful hotels and casinos, Fort Fincastle, Pirates of Nassau museum, the Queen staircase, a flower garden and the straw market. We met a sailing couple we knew from the previous year. They were on their way to Georgetown in the Great Exuma. Their plan was to spend the winter there playing games on Stocking Island, relaxing and doing absolutely nothing.

While we were in the harbor a dive boat returned from a dive. Everyone on the boat was a tourist. As they pulled to the dock an ambulance was there waiting for them. They carried one man off the dive boat in a gurney. We later learned that he had died. He had never had a dive lesson in his life and did not survive his first attempt at diving. Diving is so much fun and so exciting. The ocean floor is a new world, you cannot see enough, and every second you look you see something different. But, you must take the course, pass it and be certified.

When the weather and wind cooperated we motored out of the harbor, set sail, and stopped seven hours later at an uninhabited island called Great Guana Cay. We had to go from the ocean through a cut in the reef and then into an open Bay. We anchored, ate a meal and went to bed. The next day it was time to go ashore to explore. The shore line was a long flat stone for about six feet in, and then it was sand into the island. We saw a lot of little tracks and big tracks in the sand. We thought they might be crabs and birds. Once you left the shore area you would be in a very thick jungle. We found what looked like a stone path from the days the island was inhabited. Don cut a long stick of wood to move back and forth to swipe spiders away and we started walking. We saw a few old rotting homes that had caved in and an old cistern that also caved in. There were birds that chattered at us as we passed by and we saw several colorful eight to ten inch long lizards. It was quite mysterious to be on a foreign island with so many unusual sounds and other sensations. It was mesmerizing. The air you breathe was so clean from the ocean and throughout the jungle. We found a couple long feathers which were white with bright colors in them but could not identify the bird it came from.

When we were sailing out in the ocean and opened a can of something for lunch, Don cuts the bottom out crushed the can and throws it overboard. That is not polluting. In thirty days, the salt water totally destroys it. We kept the paper and plastic goods until we reached an island like this and burned it at low tide. While at Guana Cay, we were in the process of burning our paper and plastic when we heard a sound behind us. We turned around and found a five foot iguana watching us. That was a lifelong memory! Exciting! Fun! But definitely different from ranch life.

We stopped at one island that we thought was uninhabited until we saw a pig. It was not a wild pig but reasonably friendly. We walked through the jungle on a small path for about a mile until we arrived at the other side of the island. There we found a small settlement of about fifty people. We talked and asked them about the pig. They informed us that someone from another island dropped it off some years ago when it was just a little piglet. Since then it has walked all over the island eating roots and anything it can find. They see it about once a month.

We noticed that there were no children on most of the islands and asked why. We were told that the children are sent to live with family or friends on a larger island to attend school.

The weather was not good for sailing and that gave us time to talk and think back about when we first started sailing. I was still a ranch girl, a cowgirl. After subsequent trips, I eventually became a sailor. Another decision was when we first embarked on a life of sailing we didn't know what jobs either of us could do best in an emergency. After trial and error for a month we concluded that I would man the helm/wheel and Don would do the sails and the anchor.

We stayed on our boat near that island about ten days. When the wind came from the right direction we set sail for Georgetown in the Great Exuma. Two days later we arrived. A storm came in from the north and the wind blew for five days. It was cold and nasty with the temperature down to sixty five degrees. I thought I would freeze. We had two anchors out and were safe but were confined to the boat.

We spent a month in Georgetown harbor, walking, playing games with other sailors, attended service in the Baptist Church and had lunch with them following the service. The young boys wanted Don to take them out for a dinghy ride after lunch. He took four the first time and went out in the bay for about five minutes then brought them back and picked up four more. He continued to take the children for dinghy rides until church service started again in the afternoon.

Everyone on the island was very friendly and loved to talk and visit with us. One morning we took our dinghy to make a purchase from their grocery store. As we walked past their local school, we noticed all the children were lined up and the principal was praying for the children, the school, and for their country. When he had finished, I remarked to one of the teachers how impressive it was to witness a principal praying with the students. He said yes. We can still pray in our country. I know that you cannot in America and that is too bad. Everyone needs prayer and the love of God.

As we sailed and visited many islands, we found that in many cases, all they have is God. There is no work and nothing grew on most islands except hardwood shrubs, palm trees and mangrove trees. Although during the slave days they did grow cotton trees and onions on some islands. Banana trees were growing on one island we visited. We never heard of cotton trees before, but there were some still standing on this island. When slavery was abolished the slave owners turned the island over to the salves to do with it as they liked. Most salve owners returned to their home country. In a few years most of the salves migrated to the big cities.

Sometimes humorous things occurred in our boat. Toilets are flushed with salt water. The toilet has a valve/lever on it that you open when flushing it. Then you have to close it after you flush it or salt water keeps running in. One night I went to the bathroom and forgot to put the lever back to stop the water from coming in. A couple hours later Don went in the bathroom. Not being totally awake, he found himself standing in cold salt water. That didn't faze him but when he sat down on the toilet, he really screamed. I was just lying there in the bed and I knew what had happened. I couldn't keep from laughing. Needless to say, he was suddenly wide awake. He asked me, did you do that on purpose? I answered, No, I just forgot to shift the valve closed and continued to laugh.

From there we sailed to Little Exuma. We met a very talented older lady known locally as the Shark Lady. We talked with her and she showed us the jewelry she made from shark bones, shark teeth and stones. She showed us her relatively small boat that she uses to go out into the ocean to catch sharks. She and her friends eat the shark meat and she uses the bones and teeth to make jewelry. I bought a beautiful necklace she made. I really wanted a ring like the one she was wearing. She told me to come back in a month and she would have one made for me. I told her to make me a very nice one and I would come back the next year to buy it. That is what we did. She remembered us and had my ring ready. It is truly beautiful, I treasure it.

Don looked at our charts and had a great desire to go further south however, we had been playing around too long. In a few months it would be hurricane season and we were still in the hurricane zone, so the decision was made to head for the States and try to go farther next year.

On our way back to the States we stopped at Long Cay. The water near the island was not deep enough for us to go within a mile or two of the island so we were forced to anchor out and took our dinghy in. I don't know how many people lived on the island. We only saw and talked to three. All they had was a small store. Stores on these islands were supplied by the government. Every week or two a government boat will stop at each inhabited island and deliver meat, vegetables and other items they need. We spent about half an hour walking on the island and then got back in our dinghy and returned to our boat.

We sailed to Cat Island. Since there was not much to do there, we went fishing and diving for conch. Then we were forced to ride out a storm in the lee of the island. Most storms last only for a day or two. HF radio channels will give you reliable weather information on the time and strength of a storm and when it will hit a given area. That will give you enough time to seek shelter in the lee of an island, bury two anchors and ride out the storm.

Don once tried to bake bread under storm conditions but with the boat bouncing around it didn't rise very well, but we ate it anyway. That was the only time he had bad luck with baking bread. He did all the baking and I did the cooking.

Our stove used alcohol instead of gas or electricity. Before using the stove, air must be pumped into the alcohol tank using a bicycle pump. After running about a teaspoon of alcohol into a little trough under the burner, the alcohol can be lighted. When the burner is hot, it will light by itself.

From there we sailed to Conception Island. The diving and snorkeling were really great there. I saw a variety of very beautiful angel fish. Don caught a couple lobsters and he brought up some interesting shells. They were still living so we chose not to keep them. He also found a very large star fish, the largest he ever saw. It looked like it was twelve to fourteen inches across. Don just wanted to show me how pretty things on the ocean floor were, and then he returned them to where he found them. After I snorkeled for a while, I fished with my rod and reel and caught a big yellow tail snapper fish. It was big enough for two meals. We had books that identified fish, shells or mussels and birds.

One island we stopped at was small but very high. Over the years sailors made a little step path in the stone to the top. On top there was a stone monument and a mail box. Sailors would write a little note and put it in the mail box for other sailors to read. There were about one hundred notes in it from people all over the states and sailors from around the World.

Before the hurricane season began and we headed for home, we decided to stop at one more island to visit with the natives and sightsee or explore. That island was full of hermit crabs. They were from one inch to two inches long. Hermit crabs don't have a shell of their own so to protect their body they crawl into a sea shell. As they grow larger they need to find a larger sea shell or something they will fit in. We saw one crab with a very small glass jar that it used instead of a sea shell. We took one hermit crab with us. Don made a one foot square screen cage for it so it could crawl around. We feed it peanut butter and vegetables. We also took along several different size empty sea shells for it to grow into. We had it for two years then gave it to a second grade school teacher. Three years later we asked her if she still had it. She said, yes and all the students in that school had seen it. She was sure that her students will talk about it for years to come.

After that experience we sailed on the Chub Cay to clear customs and waited for favorable weather before making our crossing back to the states.

Very often we had to sail at night. It was always beautiful and exciting. When there was a full moon it was bright and clear enough to read a newspaper. When there was no moon the sky was full of stars, and so very bright and close it seemed as though they were only a fingertip away. There are also florescent sea creatures. The wave action from our boat disturbed them and they would make a colorful light. Sometimes a flying fish would land on the deck of the boat during the night and we would find it in the morning. We also saw them in the daytime but they never landed on our boat. They have long wing-like fins and are able to fly up to forty miles per hour for one hundred and sixty feet to escape a predator. We didn't eat them, but they are a delicacy for people in other counties.

We met and talked with a native lady on one island we visited and she told us that the land crab was good with rice. She offered to make some for us. We declined but tried it on our boat. Neither of us liked it. Don refers to food such as that as survival food.

That reminds me of the time I wanted some red meat. Don can live on sea food but occasionally I need some red meat. After all, I am a rancher. The next inhabited island we came to, we went ashore and bought some red meat at their store. When I cooked it, the smell was terrible and the taste was worse than the smell. I threw it overboard and the fish would not eat it. Don teased me. He said it was day old monkey meat.

One day I caught a mai mai or dolphin that was forty six inches long. What a fight he gave me. It took me almost half an hour to land him. We cut steaks from him and for several days he was our dinner.

The sun sets were always phenomenal. Every night we would sit in the cockpit and watch the sunset. I think Don took over a hundred sunset pictures. There was nothing to obstruct the view. You could actually see the sun go under the ocean.

The crossing was uneventful. I was glad to be home but I miss sailing already. It was so much Fun! Exciting! Peaceful! Rewarding.

Chapter "48"

Back in Key West our boating friends welcomed us back to the Bay. After we were anchored and had secured our boat, we took our dinghy to the marina for happy hour. The first thing they told us was bad news. A couple we were very close to and planned to sail with next year had a very bad accident. The couple set sail this year later than they had planned because of health problems. They returned after only two months due to the same problem. Upon their return they tied up at the dock and he went for a bicycle ride. He was on the bike path next to the main rood. A young mother looking in the back seat at her child ran off the road, run over our friend and killed him. He had served thirty two years in the Army, lived through two wars as an infantryman, sailed for five years with his wife and was killed while riding his bicycle. A few years earlier I had talked to him and his wife about the end time and they told me that they were saved. I can only hope.

We couldn't wait to launder our bed sheets and clothes. While the clothes were washing we took a shower with unlimited hot water in a shower room that was six feet square. That was always a good reason for coming home. It was heavenly. I could become a landlubber once again.

The next day we drove our truck to town. Again, Don could not drive faster than twenty miles an hour for a few miles. It was just too fast after sailing at five to six miles per hour or sometimes less. After being on the boat for six months it was difficult to walk on land or drive the truck. For a few minutes after disembarking you walk like a drunk. Life from the sea to land is quite a change. It even takes time to adjust to the surroundings. On one of our return trips, after we had anchored we went square dancing. When the caller said left allemande, Don turned to his corner, missed her by three feet and almost fell down. They thought he was drunk and didn't want to dance with him. After he explained to them that they had just returned from a seven month sail, they let him dance.

We continued to live on our boat for two weeks until we took our Airstream out of storage. Then it was off to visit our families in Washington, DC, Wyoming and Minnesota. It felt good to be back with family and friends. Our sailing trips were the main topic of our conversations with both family and friends. Then they would say, I don't know how you could do that. We showed them our pictures. They could not understand how a ranch lady could live happily out in the middle of the ocean!!!

Our activities this summer were about the same as previous summers, except Don made the navigation table for the boat that he planned. The one thing different about being in one location for a while is, we get mail every day. We have a mail service in Key West that collects our mail. When we notify them of our location and address, the service puts all of our mail in a big envelope and mails it to us. When we sailed we got our mail once in New Providence and once in the Great Exuma. After visiting, eating and playing cards with our families and friends, we were ready to head back to Key West and the Queen Bee.

Chapter "49"

It was good to be back on the Queen Bee. The weather was hot and having no air conditioning, we wore very little clothing unless we had to go to the marina or to town.

We had been living on our sailboat and sailing for six years. We had seen so much and had done even more. I am seventy years old and Don was close behind me. We could handle the boat under normal conditions but in a storm and there were many of them year round, we had to work fast, think fast and be strong. We discussed it and decided that we would sail for one more year, do as much, see as much, and visit as many islands as we could and then put our boat up for sale.

Don made arrangements to have our boat hauled out for the annual service and bottom paint. I did the bright work and the teak. When the bottom was cleaned and painted and the teak and bright work was finished, Don called to me, it's your turn to go up the mast. My answer to him was: cowgirls don't go up a fifty foot mast. I winched him up. When he was finished working,

I was a good and loyal wife and brought him down easily and slowly without any foolishness. This time it only took us six days and the Queen Bee looked great. It was time to put her back in the water and plan our trip.

Because this would be our last trip we wanted to leave the states before Christmas and stop in at as many islands as we could. It was the first of November and we and the Queen Bee are ready to sail. Don had plotted the course we would take. I prayed for good winds because Don started the engine only when he absolutely had to do so. He was a sailor not a motorman. The only time he willingly used the motor was to go into and out of customs.

We left Key West in the morning and stopped at Bahia Honda, thirty five miles east of Key West because the wind was coming from the wrong direction. It was a beautiful place. We anchored between the new and old bridge and stayed overnight. The next morning the wind had improved but was not perfect. By noon it was better so we set sail again and made our crossing through the Gulf Stream. We had a full moon with not a cloud in the crystal clear sky. I could have read my book by moonlight.

We anchored at South Riding Rock to dive for conch. No lobster this time. We cleaned the conch, slept there overnight and set sail the next morning. Sailing across crystal clear water that is only about thirty to forty feet deep is such a pleasure. I just sat there and gazed into the depths of the sea as we sailed and admired all the sea life knowing it was God's work. Man could never create such beauty. That day we sailed to Chub Cay to clear customs and emigrations. The cost was usually around one hundred dollars and is valid for one year. It includes a sailing and fishing permit. While sailing we spend about twenty five dollars a month, primarily for fresh vegetables and drinking water.

The weather and wind was still cooperative so we continued on to New Providence Island. We anchored in the bay and used our dinghy to go ashore. We ate in a local restaurant and walked around for exercise. The next day we walked over a long bridge to Paradise Island. That experience was worth a million dollars. After our walk across the long bridge we walked across a rope bridge, then through a glass tunnel with fish and other sea life swimming on top and on both sides of us. It was breath taking just to stand there and watch all the sea life swim around. There were sharks, lobsters, angel fish of all kinds, and a hundred different kinds of other fish, really breath taking. It was similar to what we see when we snorkel or dive. The beach was pristine, one of the best I have ever seen. It was developed for the resort with sand brought in from the ocean. There was a very large hotel with a night club and a casino booming with business. It appeared to me that the tourists couldn't wait to give their money away.

We anchored in that bay for ten days to have fun and to ride out a winter storm, bigger than was normal. The second night of the storm a boat was calling on the radio for help. I could tell from what they were saying that they should have never taken such a boat out in the ocean. In addition to that, they knew nothing about sailing. We were having fifty mile an hour wind with heavy rain and it was night, very dark. They were fighting that storm and coming in on the wrong side of the island, the windward side. About ten of us heard them but there was nothing we could do to help. At four o'clock in the morning they lost their boat. It ended up on the beach, in the rocks, destroyed. The local police put them in a hotel for the night. The next day several sailors worked with them, but their boat was a total lose. Hopefully they were insured.

After the storm we set sail for Allen Cay. That Island was full of iguanas. They varied in sizes from six inches to five feet long. Because they are protected by the government, they were so tame you could almost touch them. Don warned me, that before thinking about touching them, to look at their big sharp teeth and remember that they are wild animals.

From there we sailed to Hi Born Cay, Big Majors, Galliet, Muska and several other islands, exploring and visiting with the natives. On one island we met a bush doctor. We talked with him for over an hour. He told us about the medicines he concocted for his people and the leaves they used for plates when eating. He took care of the medical needs of all the people on the island but once a year the government sent a Nurse to check on the people. He said she was just wasting her time because he takes care of his people. He was very interesting to talk with but I knew there were people who wanted to see him so after more than an hour of conversation we returned to our boat. The population on the island was about one hundred he said.

Another Island we stopped at had a steep hill or small mountain about eight hundred feet high. It was solid rock same as the island, just as all the other islands we visited. On top of the hill was a small building. When we landed on the island about five or six men came to welcome us. On all the islands we visited the people were always friendly and were curious about our boat, the United States and any other subject that came to their minds. When I asked about the little house on the hill they all wanted to talk at once. We were there all day talking, listening, and visiting with them and then going up the hill to look at the house.

They told us that years ago a little priest came to their island by boat. After a few days he went up the hill and began building the house. First he had made steps in the rock to get to the top. Because he was small and had little feet, the steps were only about six inches wide, not very deep or long and nearly straight up. The entire hill was stone so he had to cut all the steps with some kind of tool. Then he started collecting stones and material to make mortar. Finally, he was ready to build this little house. When we saw it, it had three very small rooms without doors and big open spaces for windows. The entrance and inside doorways were about five feet high and two feet wide. It had three rooms about eight feet square and a flat roof. The complete building was made from stone with mortar he made. There was a small cistern to collect rain water. He lived in it for a short time and then left the island. No one knows exactly when he left or where he went. The building had survived several hurricanes and remains just as he built it.

When we decided to visit another island, we misjudged the wind. We anchored off about a quarter of a mile which was normal due of the depth of the water. We got in our dinghy, went ashore, and the wind blew us completely up on shore. When we wanted to leave the wind was still blowing. Don was in the dinghy and would start the engine as soon as we had one foot of water. I pushed the dinghy, got wet up to my ears and only got in a few inches of water, when a wave put us back on shore. A native saw what we were trying to do and came to help. He told me to get in the dinghy. I did and he pushed us out, Don started the engine and we were on our way back to the Queen Bee, wet but happy.

We found it difficult to leave some of the islands we visited. The people were very curious and friendly. Several times we tried to buy bananas and vegetables but many of the islands had nothing. We always wondered how they lived and stayed so healthy and happy. One store we went to had a large box of corn flakes with a very large live cat sitting on top of it. They had some other items in cans and boxes that we didn't need or wouldn't buy if we did need them. The place wasn't very clean but that is the way the Islanders live. One reason was because the wind blows continually and the windows and doors are always open for fresh cool air. The store was three miles from where we anchored so at least we got some exercise. We saw only four people on the island. They were friendly, but had nothing to do.

The next day we were sailing out in the ocean

miles from shore going about five knots. I was
fishing from the port side, looking at the clear
blue water with about two foot waves and to the
sky with its white puffy clouds, and then my eyes
drifted to the bow of the boat. "I screamed,
Don!!" "We are on a collision course with a
whale." Don jumped up, looked ahead of the bow
and immediately took evasive action. He started
the engine and gave full power to starboard with
the sails flapping. Then while he was putting on
his life jacket, he told me to put mine on because
whales have been known to tip sailboats over.
Five minutes later we passed a fifty foot whale
with only about three hundred feet between us.
Over the years, we have seen big fishing and
lobster boats and ships of all sizes but this is the
first whale.

Visiting all these Islands was very interesting
and enjoyable. This was our last sailing trip and
we knew we would really miss sailing and
visiting the islands and all these friendly people
with whom we had made friends with. The
people on the small islands always invited us to
come back and visit again. We should have
started sailing earlier in life.

Several young sailing couples traveled with their children. They home schooled their children and sailed just as we did, staying on some islands for several months. Their children were like fish. After school they would swim and play in the water or take their dinghy to shore and walk or play. We talked to some of the children. They ranged in age from seven to seventeen and were very intelligent. We talked to a medical doctor that home schooled his daughter on their boat and when they tried to enroll her in a medical school she was denied entry because she had been home schooled on a boat for her high school years. They returned to the states for several years until she was accepted to medical school then stated sailing again.

We met and talked to a lot of sailors with very interesting back grounds and from countries around the world. No one was on welfare, disabled or poor. They worked hard all their lives and made good plans for their retirement years. Most of the larger sea going boats we encountered were worth about one hundred thousand dollars or more. Many of the cheaper boats only sailed for a few days and returned to the states. In a few cases, after a few days at sea the women had enough and they returned. On one boat the lady flew back and left her husband and their dog on the boat.

Chapter "50"

We returned to Key West knowing this was our last trip. I have mixed feelings about it. I was a ranch girl in my heart but sailing had stolen a part of it. Because we stayed out to sea and sailed longer than usual, the hurricane season had already started. Rather than going north for the summer we agreed to stay on the boat for the remainder of the summer. We had our marina friends, our church friends, and our square dance friends. What more could we want.

We became friends with a single sailor from Virginia. He wanted us to sail up the inland waterway in the spring with him. We had never done that. I think it sounded exciting but Don said it sounded boring. To do the waterway, much of the trip would be by motor and Don is a sailor. I decided to try to convince him it would be fun to do. I have enjoyed sailing but I thought the time had come to sell the Queen Bee. We probably could sell it in Virginia just as easily as here in Key West.

We stayed busy the remainder of the summer participating in all the activities. We spent Christmas with our sailing friends, our church family and square dance friends. Soon it was time to have our boat hauled out to do the annual service.

Don had not warmed up to a trip up the waterway but reluctantly consented and began preparing by buying a guide book and charts.

It was the middle of April in Key West. The weather was perfect, warm with temperatures in the high seventies and low eighties. Our single sailing friend assured us it would be warm going up the waterway to Virginia. I was prepared and excited. This would be another new experience. Don was not thrilled about the whole idea, but would try his best to enjoy it. He already bought a guide book and plotting a course wasn't necessary. You just stay in the waterway. He knew from the guide book when the bridges would be open, information on the tides and other information pertinent to making this trip.

We left Key West and sailed for four hours. Then the time came to start the engine. We used the engine until we anchored for the night. We had supper, played a game of cards, and went to bed. The next day we traveled under motor all day and went under bridges without event. There wasn't much to see but it was different than sailing out in the ocean. The third day we motored up the waterway through Miami. That was different. We saw those beautiful new buildings with their glassy facades reaching toward the sky. The million dollar homes on the water front were palatial and beautiful. What a lavish life style they must have.

Every day we motored. We had to go under bridges or through swing bridges. We always anchored out at night and on the third or fourth evening after anchoring we would take our dinghy in to a marina. We would walk and shop then go back to the marina where we would take a shower. Most of the time, the use of the dinghy dock and a shower cost five dollars.

Half way to Virginia the weather turned cold. I had enough clothes to keep me warm but Don wore everything he owned and was still cold. He was not a happy camper or sailor. Every day he was cold and every day my sailor husband traveled unhappily under motor. He never put up the sails one time for over a month. One night just two days out of Virginia, Don didn't check his tide book. He was used to four or five foot tides. Because he couldn't sail he was not happy or thinking clearly. Traveling north the tides increase and that night when we anchored, we had ten feet of water under us. We ate supper, visited with our single friend for a while and went to bed. When we woke up our boat was lying on its side in six inches of water. What a surprise! I should say what a shock!! We looked at each other and burst out laughing. There was nothing else to do but laugh and wait for the tide to come in. When it did come in we started the engine and motored up the waterway. Don said, this is not our best trip and I knew it was best that I remain silent on that subject.

We arrived in Norfolk, Virginia in the afternoon and tied up to the dock in a marina. We walked around and checked the place out. When returned to the boat, Don saw the sides of our boat and almost screamed. When we left Key West our boat was clean and shiny. Now it is rust colored from the waterway water. He spent three days working from the dinghy cleaning it. When he was finished he looked at me and said, "Now I'm ready to sell it."

The next day he contacted all the big boat catalog companies that advertise boats for sale. Some catalogs were published every six months and others once a year. A boat like ours was difficult to sell because of the cost and the only a person interested in our boat would be a person who wants to sail out in the ocean and maybe around the world. We decided to rest here for a few days and then set sail for New Jersey and New York to see the Statue of Liberty and other sights and then sail back here and wait for a buyer. Don remarked, just to cover all bases I will put an ad in the local paper.

The next day, about a half hour after we were out of bed and before breakfast, the telephone rang. It was from a man who saw the ad in the local paper and wanted to see our boat. I asked him when he wanted to see it. He replied, in half an hour if that is all right with you. I answered sure, come on over. I gave him directions to our boat. He arrived in a business suit and looked very distinguished. We showed him our boat and after a short conversation he said he liked it and wanted his wife to see it. The next morning at the same time he and his wife arrived and looked over our boat. He eventually asked what our bottom price would be. Our asking price was listed in the paper. We dropped our price one thousand dollars and added that we would not take a penny less. He asked for time to think about it and would get back to us later. That noon he called us to say they would buy it, and they would come over tomorrow morning at eight with a contract and a down payment. A boat that size and documented must be surveyed before a sale can be closed. I offered to make arrangements for the survey and would let him know tomorrow when he arrives when and where it will be.

It was ten days before we could get the boatyard and the surveyor together, so Don took a flight back to Key West to get our truck and Airstream trailer which was in storage. When he arrived here, he put it in an RV Park near the marina.

We had our boat hauled out at a local boatyard. When the surveyor arrived we talked and joked. He warned me that when he was finished I wouldn't be smiling. He had been surveying boats for twenty years and none had passed one hundred percent. It took him an entire day to complete the job. When he was finished he showed us a blank sheet of paper with his letterhead on top. He found absolutely no defects and that he has never seen a boat in such excellent condition.

We put the boat back in the water and asked the buyers if they would like to go for a sail the next Saturday. They enthusiastically consented.

Saturday we went out in the bay for a sail and they thoroughly enjoyed it. As they left he said I'll call you. The next day he called and asked if we would take cash. I said, you mean green money? He answered Yes. Our phone was on speaker mode. I looked at Don. Don said, Yes, as long as it is spendable money. Then he asked, "Where can we make the transfer." I answered, how about in our boat. A few minutes after the phone call we started talking about it. That was a pile of cash money to be exchanged in our boat? I called a local bank explaining to them about the exchange of a large sum of money and asked if we could make the transfer at the bank and open an account. I also asked if they could count money fast! They answered both questions in the affirmative. I called the new buyer and gave him the information. We agreed to meet at noon the next day. At twelve o'clock Don and I were in the bank with the bank president, a young lady cashier and an empty room with a very large table. Then we waited. Five minutes after twelve a bright red convertible pulled up to the bank. The gentleman got out of the driver's seat, walked around to the passenger side, opened the door, and took out a very large shopping bag with handles and a towel on top. We met him at the bank door and walked with him to the empty room where he dumped all the money on the table. There was so much that some fell on the floor. The cashier started marking and counting. She was fast but it still took over half an hour. There were a few twenties and the remainder was in fifties and hundreds, all perfectly good money. When we finished and the boat was his, he said I suppose you are wondering where I got this cash money. "We said," Yes, we were curious because you certainly didn't look like someone in the drug world. He laughed and informed us that he was a plastic surgeon and every dime he put in the bank, his ex-wife knew about it and wanted her part. When his patients paid in cash he put it in his safe so someday he could buy a sailboat. Today was that day.

There is a saying that goes; there are two happy days in a boat owner's life. The day he buys the boat and the day he sells it. That was not true with us. As we walked away from our sailboat, our home, our Queen Bee we both had a little tear in our eyes. We had just said good-bye to many exciting times, exotic places, interesting people, and the Queen Bee. Being true optimists as we were, we knew more exciting and different things lay ahead for us.

Chapter "51"

We moved into our Airstream and stayed in the RV Park for a few days. At this point in our lives we weren't too sure what we wanted to do. We traveled to Washington, DC to visit family and friends, then to the ranch in Wyoming, and on to Minnesota to visit family. When the weather turned cold, we headed for Florida. We stopped at the Melbourne Airstream Park and planned to stay a day or two. We went square dancing, ate out, and attend service at the Baptist Church. Everybody we met was very cordial and friendly so we decided to stay a few days longer. The longer we were there the more we enjoyed it so that is where we decided to spend the winter. It didn't take long for Don and me to become involved in the church and began to meet more people in church and square dancing. There were three square dance clubs in the Melbourne area and we chose to dance with all three. Six months later we became more involved in the church. Once again I found myself working in the nursery and being known as the rocking grandmother. Don was an usher, greeter and assisted in counting the money/offering and other jobs the Pastor asked him to do.

The square dance club we danced with the most asked Don and me to run for president of the club. We ran and were elected to serve for one year. It was an average sized club, but with Don's management, jokes, and foolishness, the club increased in size by fifty percent. By the end of our year the membership wanted to elect us as permanent presidents. We declined but continued to assist wherever we were needed.

For the next three years we lived in our Airstream and in the Park. In the summer we went north as usual for a few months. In the winter the park was filled with winter people, known as snowbirds. They enjoyed playing card games and other table games. I loved it because I could play anything they wanted me to play.

The park was a corporation, run by a board of directors elected by the stock holders which included us. After we lived there for several years, Don was asked to run for the Board. We discussed it and agreed that he should run. When the ballots were counted, he was elected vice president having received seventy percent of the votes. I mentioned to Don that I didn't want to sit around without him and do nothing. The next day he said the job of Postmistress was open. He added that if I took the job, I would have three hundred mail boxes to service and would have only one helper. I accepted the job and loved it. I kept the call window open for four hours, six days a week and came to know most of the people in the park. They were so friendly to me. Some of the men always told a joke or teased me about something.. Don served as vice president for three years until the President retired. Then Don became President. Two years later we both retired from our respective positions.

I missed seeing all my friends every day but Don admitted he had no training for that type of business and was happy to be away from it.

Don decided he wanted a garden and we both agreed we wanted a house and home. We drove all over Georgia, South Carolina and the southern part of Tennessee. We finally decided to settle in South Carolina. We bought a nice home in Westminster on one acre of land. We enjoyed our new home, the summer, our flowers, and the vegetable garden but the winter was colder than we had expected. We spent the next summer there and then bought a house in Melbourne, Florida where we could spend the winters. We were happy with that arrangement for three years. Then we found a really good Baptist Church and a very good square dance club in Anderson South Carolina. We believe the preaching and the music in that Baptist Church was the best we ever heard. We decided to sell our home in Florida and in Westminster, buy a home in Anderson, and spend the summers there and the winters in our Airstream in Melbourne Florida. We bought a large home in Anderson with a sizable yard, a large enclosed RV garage and it was located in a respectable neighborhood. After we closed on our house I asked Don, "Can I unpack my bags now?" He assured me, "Yes this will be our last house." Knowing Don I wasn't too sure if I could believe that or not. Our new home was in very good condition so I don't know if he would find something to change. Previously, we always renovated our homes and improved the landscapes which yielded us substantial profits when we sole them. When we bought them Don called them, handyman specials.

Don has a beautiful vegetable garden, and we both work in the flowerbeds around the house. We have a grape vine and a fig tree. We discussed about planting a pecan tree and a few fruit trees since they grow easily here, but decided against it. We have enough to do.

We enjoy all of our new friends at church and in the square dance club. There are yard and garden stores for Don, and a variety of other stores for me. There are also a variety of restaurants where we enjoy eating. Don's garden, yard, and workshop keep him busy. He has made about ten birdhouses. We have a bird bath that the birds love, and we love observing them as they flutter around in the water. We have attracted all kinds of birds that enjoy eating the bugs that plaque our plants. The houses are fully occupied in the spring and some choose to spend the entire summer with us.

When we bought our home, there was a mother-in-law house in the back yard. Don converted it to a playhouse for me. I now have all my arts and crafts in one place. Seventeen years ago I began making a bedspread, designed with all fifty state birds and state flowers embroidered on it. Each one is on a nine inch square. Before, during, and after my boating life, whenever I had free time I would work on my spread. I have finished it, and my friends have declared it a work of art. At first I didn't want to use it because it was so beautiful, but Don insisted that we use it because I made it. Now I am in a dilemma: To which child, grandchild, or great grandchild shall I will it. A good friend suggested that I leave it to a museum. That's something for me to consider.

Another thing I do in my playhouse is ceramics. I have made several different Indian heads, a large eagle, and other birds. I have also fashioned Indian heads with crewel. I have made counted cross stitch samplers for my twenty-five great grandchildren and my twelve grandchildren. I painted birds with acrylics on barn wood and drift wood that we collected from the ocean in our sailing days. When I need a change of pace I put puzzles together. Two were so beautiful that I put glue on them and Don made nice wood frames. I also craft special gifts for my friends. One craft I do in counted cross stitch on a two by four inch adia cloth is a little thing with a magnet on the back saying "Sending you a Hug." Another project I make on four by six inch adia cloth with a magnet for the dish washer saying "Clean" on one side and when you turn it over it reads "Dirty."

One day in the spring of the year I put a flowered wreath on my playhouse door. The next day a Robin built her nest in it. Then she laid her eggs in it. We watched the eggs hatch and the babies grow but didn't have the heart to disturb her so I didn't use my playhouse until the babies were grown and blew away.

Don wrote three books. The title of the first one which was digital only is: My years as CIA undercover agent. The title of the second is: The Insider, CIA to the White House and the third, which is this one, is: Saddle to Sailboat. The first one he discontinued because he used some of it in the second. The last two are available from Amazon as a digital and printed book. When we go to Wyoming and Minnesota we take along thirty five or forty books. When old friends and school mates hear that he wrote and had published a book, they had to buy a copy. By the time we got home he was sold out. Some ordered the digital copy from Amazon.

About a year ago it happened. Don came home from visiting a friend and said he had found a beautiful little home with two bedrooms and a small yard in a good respectable neighborhood. He asked me, what do you think? You want to look at it? I promptly answered; you can buy it and live in it. When you get hungry you can come visit me because I'm not moving again. That ended that subject. We have lived in this house for sixteen years. I just knew he would be getting itchy feet. He loves it here as much as I do, so I think he was just teasing me. He still square and round dances and is always busy in the yard, the garden and his workshop plus his work for the church. We both feel well and owe our health to eating what medical science claims is good for us plus we exercise regularly. The first thing we do after we get up in the morning is thirty minutes of stretching exercises. Then Don walks over a mile and I walk around the block.

We reminisce about our sailboat and the pleasure we had sailing, the places we visited, and the people we met. Sometime I think of my first day in Florida when the boat salesman wanted to sell me a sailboat. Me! a Wyoming rancher wearing western riding boots. In my wildest imagination did I know that someday I would own a sailboat and sail the deep blue seas of the Atlantic Ocean. Despite all those wonderful things, we do not plan to repeat any of our previous activities because we still have things to do and experience. Don is eighty seven and I am ninety two. We still make plans to travel or do something different. We left our Airstream in the Airstream RV Park in Florida and have bought a little Motorhome. It has a generator and everything that the Queen Bee had. Traveling and living in it for a week or a month should be fun.

Made in the USA
Columbia, SC
04 August 2018